THE LANGUAGE OF THE SPIRIT
INTERPRETING AND TRANSLATING CHARISMATIC TERMS

THE LANGUAGE OF THE SPIRIT

INTERPRETING AND TRANSLATING CHARISMATIC TERMS

ROBERT P. MENZIES

CPT Press
Cleveland, Tennessee

The Language of the Spirit
Interpreting and Translating Charismatic Terms

Published by CPT Press
900 Walker ST NE
Cleveland, TN 37311
USA
email: cptpress@pentecostaltheology.org
website: www.cptpress.com

Library of Congress Control Number: 2010936907

ISBN-10: 1935931016
ISBN-13: 9781935931010

The Graeca font used to print this work is available from Linguist's Software, Inc., PO Box 580, Edmonds, WA 98020-0580 USA tel (425) 775-1130 www.linguistsoftware.com.

BWHEBB, BWHEBL, BWTRANSH [Hebrew]; BWGRKL, BWGRKN, and BWGRKI [Greek] Postscript® Type 1 and TrueTypeT fonts Copyright © 1994-2009 BibleWorks, LLC. All rights reserved. These Biblical Greek and Hebrew fonts are used with permission and are from BibleWorks, software for Biblical exegesis and research.

DEDICATION

To a group of friends, colleagues, and counselors who have enabled my service in China and made it a joy: Tim Dresselhaus, Tod Eastlake, Joe Elliot, Dave Gable, Del Guynes, Ron Johnson, Jonathan Logan, William Menzies, Lance Stoddart, Matt Wells.

CONTENTS

PREFACE

In addition to the group noted in the dedication, a number of others have helped make the publication of this book a reality. I would like to thank Paul Li for his help with Chinese sources and terms. Paul has been a wonderful friend over the years and without his friendship and encouragement I doubt that I would still be serving in China. I would also like to thank another good friend, Grant Hochman, and my father, William Menzies. Both read the manuscript in its entirety and offered many helpful suggestions. It has been my delight to work with John Christopher Thomas and Lee Roy Martin of CPT Press. Chris' invitation for me to give the 2008 Clarence J. Abbott Lecture in Biblical Studies at the Church of God Theological Seminary in Cleveland, TN helped stimulate many of the ideas that led to the formation of this book. I have fond memories of the rich fellowship I shared with Chris and the Church of God Theological Seminary family during that week of lectures, discussions, prayer, and worship.

Finally, I would like to thank various publishers and editors for allowing me to use excerpts from some of my previous writings: the Introduction contains a brief story also found in *Stories from China: Fried Rice for the Soul* (Milton Keynes, UK: Authentic Media, 2005), pp. 138-41; Chapter One was initially published as 'Anti-Charismatic Bias in the Chinese *Union Version* of the Bible', *Pneuma* 29 (2007), pp. 86-101; the introductory section of Chapter Two draws from and reworks portions of 'Acts 2:17-21: A Paradigm for Pentecostal Mission', *Journal of Pentecostal Theology* 17 (2008), pp. 200-18; Chapter Three is a slightly reworked version of 'John's Place in the Development of Early Christian Pneumatology', in Wonsuk Ma and Robert Menzies (eds.), *The Spirit and Spirituality: Essays in Honor of Russell P. Spittler* (JPTSup 24; Continuum, 2004), pp. 48-59; Chapter Five incorporates some material from 'The Sending of the Seventy and Luke's Purpose', in Paul Alexander, Jordan D. May, and Robert Reid (eds.), *Trajectories in the Book of Acts: Essays in Honor of John Wesley Wyckoff* (Eugene, OR: Wipf & Stock, 2010), pp. 87-113; and Chapter Six incorporates material from my review of Keith Hacking's book in *The Evangelical Quarterly*: A Review of 'Signs and Wonders, Then and Now: Miracle-working, Commissioning and Discipleship by Keith J. Hacking', *EQ* (2007), pp. 261-65. In another section of this chapter I also draw from *Empowered for Witness* (JPTSup 6; Sheffield: Sheffield Academic Press, 1994), pp. 119-22. All of this material is used with permission.

INTRODUCTION

I have a love-hate relationship with Chinese characters. On the one hand, I find in them fascinating images that often vividly portray the concepts that they seek to convey. On the other hand, they are notoriously difficult to remember and represent a huge amount of sweat and tears that, in my moments of discouragement, I know could have been avoided if the Chinese had simply created an alphabet about 3,000 years ago. I was recently reminded afresh of the power of Chinese characters to illuminate and communicate.

I had run across this interesting quote: 'Dogs are our link to paradise. They don't know evil or jealousy or discontent. To sit with a dog on a glorious afternoon is to be back in Eden, where doing nothing was not boring – it was peace'.[1] Since I am a dog lover, I shared this quote with several of my Chinese friends. They agreed that 'one dog' may be heaven, but suggested that 'two dogs' might also be hell. They then pointed out that the main character (*yu*) in the Chinese term for 'hell' (*di yu*) is composed of three parts. The left and right parts are radicals for 'dog'. The middle part is the radical for the verb 'to speak'. The Chinese character for 'hell' is thus a picture of two dogs barking (or 'speaking') at one other. It is a very vivid picture indeed.

On a more biblical note, I have always been impressed with the Chinese translation of the term, χάρισμα ('gift') in 1 Cor. 12.4. The Chinese term, *en ci*,[2] contains two characters, both full of rich

---

[1] Milan Kundera, *Guideposts* (September, 2003), p. 29.
[2] 恩賜。 This is the term utilized in the Chinese *Union Version*.

meaning. The first character, *en*, signifies God's grace.[3] The second character, *ci*, is used in connection with the giving of a gift. However, it is only used in special situations. It designates a gift that is given by one who is exalted, such as the emperor, to one who is of lower status, such as one of his subjects. Thus, together, *en ci*, paint a beautiful picture: they describe in vivid fashion gifts graciously given to us by an exalted Lord.

All languages have a special way of illustrating concepts. It has been my joy to minister in a language other than my English mother tongue for many years, Mandarin Chinese. Over the past sixteen years I have spent considerable time reading the Bible in Chinese. I have come to view this experience as a special privilege for two reasons. First, God has created every culture. He is the author of every language. Thus, each culture reflects a bit of his glory and creative power.[4] Additionally, each language represents a fresh, God-given window on the Scriptures. My encounter with the Chinese Bible and Chinese Christians has certainly challenged me to look with fresh eyes at texts that I thought were familiar and well known.

For example, during one worship service, a Chinese friend, Brother Li, shared a message from the Bible. He read the beginning of the Lord's Prayer (Mt. 6.9-13), 'Our Father in Heaven', and then asked, 'Why did Jesus start his prayer this way?' I immediately thought of God's love for us. Just as a father loves his children, so also God loves us. After a moment, Li stated that the chief reason, reflected in the next line of the prayer (in good Hebrew poetic fashion), is that, above all, we should respect and love our heavenly Father. 'Hallowed be your name' (Mt. 6.9).

It struck me how this insight came so naturally to my Chinese friends who have grown up in a culture that emphasizes respect for parents (filial piety). But for me, a Westerner, I tended to think of the father's love for his children, not of the children's love for the father. I began to think of how much closer Chinese culture is to the culture of the Bible and how significant Brother Li's point was. Yes, God loves us and this is part of the message; but

---

[3] The Chinese term thus echoes the Greek term, which also builds on the Greek word for grace, χάρις.

[4] Of course each culture also contains aspects that are fallen and distorted, and that thus need to be transformed as well.

Brother Li put the accent in the right place. The focus of the Lord's prayer is upon God. His name should be honored, exalted, and worshipped. That is the chief concern of the beginning of the Lord's prayer.

I do believe that we in the West have much to learn from Christians who live in other cultural settings and social contexts. Their unique context and experiences help them see truths in the Bible that often go unnoticed by us. Of course, the converse is also true as well. We all have our culturally induced blind spots. However, through our interaction with one another, particularly those from different settings, we can often understand God's word and ourselves more clearly. During my sojourn in China, I have found that I am not the only one who needs a new pair of glasses.

Rush hour in our city is something to behold. Thousands upon thousands of bicyclists pack into crowded bike lanes and pedal home. The number of buses and cars that clog the already congested streets has risen dramatically in the last few years, but bicycles still represent the standard mode of transportation.

One afternoon my wife and I were pedaling home on a busy street. We were part of a human current, swept along by the flow of countless bicycles. As we crossed a major intersection, we saw before us a man, clearly unconscious, sprawled on top of his toppled bicycle in the middle of the narrow, ten-foot wide, bike lane. With some difficulty, the sea of bicycles simply parted and passed around him as if nothing had happened. Not one person stopped to help. We were astounded at this callousness. We quickly dismounted and attempted to help the poor man, even as some shouted to us not to bother. After moving him to the sidewalk, I rushed over to a small clinic across the street. When I returned with a doctor and a stretcher, the man was already conscious and talking with my wife. After a brief conversation with the doctor and a word of thanks to us, he re-entered the stream of bicycles and disappeared into the distance.

It took me some time to put this incident in perspective. I had always viewed Chinese people as very gracious and hospitable. Our Chinese friends were without exception incredibly cordial hosts. Moreover, the Chinese we know value relationships with family members and friends in a way that often puts us in the West to shame. So I struggled to understand this experience.

In time, however, the matter became clear to me. There are spheres of relationship in China: family, friends, colleagues, and guests. If you fit into one of these categories, you will be treated with great kindness. However, if you do not, you essentially do not exist. The same people who are tremendously kind to their friends or guests, without giving it a second thought will pedal by an unknown bicyclist in need. Everything depends on relationship (*guanxi*).

I have pondered what is at the root of this particular cultural trait. The sheer volume of people in China tends to encourage the Chinese to compartmentalize their lives. After all, if you feel responsible for everyone, your day would be one endless series of interruptions. With people pressing in on every side, it is better to focus on those whom you know, the relationships that are clearly defined. But, it is precisely here where I see a deeper, more fundamental influence upon Chinese perceptions. Here we see the difference between Confucius and Jesus.

Not long after the bicycle incident I found myself teaching an evening course on the parables of Jesus for a group of Chinese Christians. It was exciting to see this eager group's response to these provocative and powerful stories. When we came to the parable of the Good Samaritan, I pointed out that here Jesus was addressing a question common in his day: to whom must I show compassion and concern? Does my responsibility extend to people in my family, my tribe, or my ethnic group? How large is the sphere of my responsibility? I then shared my experience in the bicycle lane with the group. Smiles came to their faces and their eyes gleamed with awareness. They knew exactly what I was talking about. We all agreed, in the Chinese context, Jesus' teaching is especially striking, especially relevant. For with this short story, Jesus declares that we cannot carefully compartmentalize our lives. He calls for us to see our sphere of responsibility in the largest possible terms. He challenges us to show compassion to those in need regardless of the nature of our relationship, regardless of the barriers that so often divide. The next time a bicyclist falls in our city, I know a group of Chinese believers who will not simply pedal on by.

I have indeed been richly blessed and often challenged by my interaction with Christianity in China. I have also encountered various texts that I feel might be translated in a manner that more clearly and accurately conveys the intent of the Biblical author. The following chapters highlight a number of these passages, particularly those that deal with the work of the Holy Spirit or charismatic themes in the New Testament.

In Chapter One the manner in which the translators of the Chinese *Union Version* translate the verb, 'to prophesy' (προφητεύω), in 1 Corinthians 12-14 is the focus of our discussion. Our analysis here has significant implications for English translations as well.

In Chapter Two I examine a number of passages where the *Union Version* translators have translated the term, πνεῦμα, as referring to the human spirit or related attitudes, when in fact the term should be understood as a reference to the Spirit of God. I suggest that the *Union Version* translators were uncomfortable with texts that refer to the Spirit of God speaking to, leading, or guiding followers of Jesus in very personal and subjective ways. This tendency can also be found in some English translations.

In Chapter Three I deal with the troublesome question, how shall we translate the term, παράκλητος? I suggest that John's pneumatology calls into question the numerous attempts to translate παράκλητος with vague, non-forensic titles. Translations such as 'comforter', 'exhorter', 'counselor', 'helper', and the Chinese *Union Version's* 'teacher' (*bao hui shi*), all miss the mark.

The kingdom of God is the subject of inquiry in Chapter Four. More specifically, I examine Jesus' declaration, 'the kingdom of God is within you' (Lk. 17.21). Although the NIV translates ἐντὸς ὑμῶν in Lk. 17.21 with the phrase, 'within you', and the Chinese *Union Version* follows a similar approach, I argue that these translations needs to be reconsidered.

In Chapter Five I deal with an interesting textual question. The manuscript evidence is divided: In Luke 10, how many disciples did Jesus send out, seventy or seventy-two? The answer to this question involves much more than simply a small change in numbers. I argue that the number conveys a significant theological point.

Finally, in Chapter Six, I examine the phrase λαλεῖν ἑτέραις γλώσσαις in Acts 2.4 and argue that 'to speak in other languages' (NRSV), a translation followed closely by the Chinese *Union Version*, is not a suitable translation. In the process, I challenge common assumptions regarding Luke's presentation of salvation history and the notion that Pentecost is the birth of the church.

I conclude with a brief summary of my findings.

I do wish to express my appreciation for the Chinese *Union Version*[5] of the New Testament and the gifted translators who labored for so long to produce this fine work. I share a bit of the story behind this amazing work in Chapter One. However, since in this book I focus on passages that, in my opinion, need to be translated in a fresh way, most of my comments in this book pertaining to the Chinese *Union Version* will necessarily be critical. In so doing I do not wish to minimize the dedication and skill of the translators of this extraordinary work.

As I have pondered the various texts discussed in this book, I have found that the issues and perspectives that I have encountered through my reading of the Chinese Bible often shed valuable light on the English translation of the New Testament as well. For this reason, I have determined to make this study available to an English-speaking audience. I do so with the hope and prayer that this work will encourage the broader Christian community as it seeks to better understand and more faithfully obey the message of the New Testament.

---

[5] In Chinese, the *He He Ben*, 和合本。

1

PROPHECY OR PREACHING?

The living room of the tiny apartment was packed with Chinese believers. The eagerness of the students and their hunger for the Word of God was truly inspiring. At this point in my ministry, I had only been in China a few years. Nevertheless, several church leaders knew of my Pentecostal orientation and my interest in the work of the Spirit. So, they asked me to speak to the group concerning the New Testament teaching on the work of the Holy Spirit.

I began by teaching about the activity of the Holy Spirit in Luke–Acts. As we looked at a number of key passages, I noted that in Luke–Acts the Spirit is, above all, the Spirit of prophecy. Throughout Luke–Acts the Spirit is presented as the source of prophetic inspiration, inspiring speech and granting special wisdom. In this way, the Spirit enables the church to bear witness for Christ, even in the face of opposition and persecution, and directs its mission. At one point, I noted that this understanding of the Spirit as the source of prophetic inspiration also forms the backdrop for what Paul refers to as 'the gift of prophecy' in 1 Corinthians 12-14. Here too Paul refers to the Spirit as the source of spontaneous, Spirit-inspired speech. When I mentioned the 'gift of prophecy' in 1 Corinthians 12-14, there was a puzzled look on the faces of a number of the believers. Then one of the bolder Chinese Christians blurted out in Mandarin Chinese, 'Paul doesn't speak of prophecy (*yu yan*)[1] in 1 Corinthians 12-14. In these verses he talks about preaching (*jiang dao*)[2]!'

I was a bit stunned by this response and suggested that we all look at 1 Cor. 14.1. I was then introduced for the first time to a peculiarity of the Chinese *Union Version*, the standard Chinese translation of the Bible that is today used by virtually all of the Christians in China. I found that the text of 1 Cor. 14.1 reads: '… eagerly desire spiritual gifts, especially prophetic preaching (*xian zhi jiang dao*)'.[3] I noticed that the term normally used for prophecy (*yu yan*) was not to be found here or elsewhere for that matter in 1 Corinthians 12-14 of the *Union Version*.[4] Instead, the translators used a phrase that is normally associated with preaching (*jiang dao*), and qualified it with the term for prophet (*xian zhi*).[5] Thus, the essential idea conveyed is that of 'prophetic preaching', with preaching being the dominant theme. Certainly in the mind of these Chinese brothers and sisters this passage had little to do with a spontaneous message inspired by the Spirit. Rather, this passage spoke of the Spirit's role in helping believers explain the meaning of the Bible after careful study of the text. In the eyes of these Chinese believers, then, 1 Cor. 14.1 encourages believers to seek the gift of preaching.

In the following essay I would like to look more carefully at this peculiarity of the Chinese *Union Version* – a peculiarity I term 'the anti-charismatic bias' of the *Union Version*. We shall first look at the history of the *Union Version* translation, which will enable us to understand better the dynamics that helped shaped this translation. We shall then look at how the translators dealt with specific texts, particularly those that support the contention that the *Union Version* reflects a clear tendency that might be termed, 'anti-charismatic'. Finally, we shall assess our findings and inquire into the motivation for this tendency.

---

[1] 预言。
[2] 讲道。
[3] 先知讲道。
[4] The one exception is found in 1 Cor. 14.6.
[5] 先知。

The History of the *Union Version* Translation of the New Testament

The translation of the Bible that has become the standard for Christians in China is termed the *Union Version*.[6] It is hard to underestimate the importance of the *Union Version* for the Chinese church, for it is used by virtually all of the Christians in China, whether they worship in the government-recognized, TSPM churches, or in house churches. In most quarters, to attempt to use another translation would be tantamount to using a text other than the Bible. Christians in China today view the *Union Version* like an earlier generation of English-speaking Christians viewed the *King James Version*. It is the Word of God and there is no other.

This important translation traces its origins back to a missionary conference that convened in Shanghai in 1890.[7] Prior to the conference there was a growing sense of need for a recognized translation of the Bible that all Protestant groups could agree upon and use. The delegates of the conference actually determined that work on three Union Versions of the Chinese Bible should be undertaken: two versions in classical or literary Chinese (High Wenli and Easy Wenli); and a *Union Mandarin Version*. Ironically, at the time most missionaries felt that the classical versions were most important, while the Mandarin version was viewed as relatively insignificant. History would prove these perceptions wrong. It was the *Union Mandarin Version* that would have a lasting and significant influence – as we have noted, an influence that still exists today. It is upon this particular project, and more particularly the translation of the New Testament into Mandarin Chinese, that we will focus.

---

[6] In Chinese, the *He He Ben*, 和合本。

[7] On the history of the *Union Version*, see Jost Zetzsche, *The Bible in China: History of the Union Version or The Culmination of Protestant Missionary Bible Translation in China* (Monumenta Serica Monograph Series 45; Nettetal: Monumenta Serica, 1999); Thor Strandenaes, *Principles of Chinese Bible Translation As Expressed in Five Selected Versions of the New Testament and Exemplified by Matthew 5.1 and Colossians 1* (Coniectanea Biblica NTS, 19; Stockhom: Almquist and Wiksell International, 1987); and Chiu Wai-boon, 'Chinese Versions of the Bible', *China Graduate School of Theology Journal* 16 (January 1994), pp. 83-95, esp. pp. 89-90. Marshall Broomhall also provides an inspirational and more popular description in his, *The Bible in China* (London: China Inland Mission and Religious Tract Society, 1934).

The translation known as the *Union Mandarin Version* (now known as and hereafter referred to as the *Union Version*) of the New Testament was produced by a committee of scholars selected and sanctioned by the Protestant Missionary Conference of 1890. An executive committee of ten members was selected by the conference, and this committee in turn selected a team of seven translators. Over the years, a variety of translators served as members of the translation team. However, three men formed the core of the translation team, significantly shaped the final product, and guided this project over the years. These men were: C.W. Mateer of the American Presbyterian Mission; Chauncey Goodrich, a Congregationalist missionary who served with the American Board of Commissioners for Foreign Missions; and F.W. Baller, a Baptist missionary associated with the China Inland Mission. These three men, uniquely qualified to engage in translation work, gave a great portion of the best years of their lives to see the project completed.[8] This was no small feat, for the entire project lasted 30 years. The project, as we have noted, was initiated in 1890. The *Union Version* of the New Testament was completed and published in 1907. A revision of this translation was published together with the completed translation of the Old Testament in 1919. This work represents the standard Chinese translation of the Bible currently used in China today, the *Union Version*. Mateer, Goodrich, and Baller were involved in a significant way at every stage of this translation of the New Testament, including the final revisions that culminated in the *Union Version* of 1919. For our purposes, it is also important to note that the key translators of the *Union Version* of the New Testament – Mateer, Goodrich, and Baller – were all steeped in the Reformed tradition.

The Protestant Missionary Conference of 1890 not only initiated the translation project by selecting the executive committee, it also laid down an important guiding principle for the project. The conference felt strongly that each of the Union Versions should

---

[8] Zetzsche, *The Bible in China*, p. 222: 'The finally assembled Mandarin translation committee consisted of three men who had given much of their lives to the promotion of Mandarin anyway – Mateer, Goodrich, and Baller – and others whose qualifications were quite limited.' On the dominant role played by these three men in the translation of the New Testament, see Zetzsche, *The Bible in China*, pp. 258-74, 322-30.

be based upon the same biblical text. With respect to the New Testament, the conference determined that the Greek text underlying the then recently published *Revised English Version* should 'be made the basis, with the privilege of any deviations in accordance with the Authorized Version'.[9] The translation team remained faithful to this guideline over the course of the project. Thus, the *Union Version* New Testament 'was based on a Greek text which generally reads like the Greek text underlying [the *Revised English Version*]', although the *Union Version* was 'more conservative' than the *Revised English Version* in keeping with readings of the *Textus Receptus*.[10]

On November 18, 1891 the translators met together with the members of the executive committees and established 18 principles which were to guide the translation project. Four are particularly important for our purposes:

3. Passages expressed in the same terms and in the same or similar connection in the original, translate in the uniform manner.

4. Translate Greek and Hebrew words occurring in different places and used in the same sense by the same Chinese words ....

11. Make a special effort to render literally words and phrases which have a theological or ethical importance, and which are, or may be, used by any school for proof or support of doctrines; putting explanations in the margin, if necessary ....

15. When two or more interpretations seem quite or nearly equally good, give one in the text and the other, or others, in the margin.[11]

These principles highlight the executive committee and the translation team's desire to translate significant Greek terms consistently (Principles #3 and 4 above) and also to translate terms of theological importance in a literal way, with a minimum of theological interpretation, so as not to alienate specific Protestant

---

[9] Zetzsche, *The Bible in China*, p. 200.
[10] Strandeneas, *Principles of Chinese Bible Translation*, p. 84.
[11] Zetzsche, *The Bible in China*, pp. 225-26.

churches (Principles #11 and 15). Let us now turn to the translation of the New Testament itself and examine how faithful the translators were to these guiding principles. Our inquiry will focus on how the *Union Version* translators rendered the term προφητεύω ('to prophesy') into Chinese.

The Translation of προφητεύω

The Chinese *Union Version* of the New Testament generally translates the Greek term, προφητεύω ('to prophesy'), with the Chinese phrase normally used to describe prophetic speech, *shuo yu yan.*[12] The character *shuo* means 'to speak'. The characters *yu yan* suggest the idea of 'speaking (*yan*) beforehand (*yu*)', thus they routinely designate prophetic speech. In this sense the phrase *yu yan* is very much like the Greek term, προφητεύω, which also suggests speaking (φημί, 'to say') beforehand (προ, 'before'). Of course the concept of prophecy in the New Testament is larger than simply predicting future events, but this is a core element of the term. The tendency for the *Union Version* to translate the verb προφητεύω ('to prophesy') with *shuo yu yan* may be illustrated with a number of texts.[13]

Matthew 11.13 reads, 'For all the Prophets and the Law prophesied until John'.[14] The Greek term translated 'prophesied' is a form of the verb προφητεύω. The Chinese text at this point translates this Greek term with the phrase *shuo yu yan.*

Similarly, Mk 14.65 describes how, shortly before the death of Jesus, 'they blindfolded him, struck him with their fists, and said, 'Prophesy!' Again, the Greek word rendered 'prophesy' is a form of the verb προφητεύω. And the Chinese text translates with the phrase *shuo yu yan.*

---

[12] 说预言。

[13] Of the 27 references to προφητεύω in the New Testament, 13 are translated with the term *yu yan*: Mt. 11.13, 15.7, Mk 7.6, 14.65, Lk. 1.67, Jn 11.51, Acts 2.17, 18, 19.6, 21.9, 1 Pet. 1.10, Jude 14, and Rev. 10.11. Two references are translated with the term *gao su* ('to tell'): Mt. 26.68 and Lk. 22.64. Twelve references are translated with terms associated with preaching: – *jiang dao* ('to preach'): 1 Cor. 11.4, 5, 13.9, 14.1, 3, 4, 5, 24, 31, 39; *chuan dao* ('to proclaim'): Mt. 7.22 and Rev. 11.3.

[14] All English Scripture citations are taken from the NIV unless otherwise noted.

The prophecy of Caiaphas is recorded in Jn 11.51, 'He did not say this on his own, but as high priest that year he prophesied that Jesus would die for the Jewish nation ....' The Greek text again employs a form of προφητεύω, which the *Union Version* translates with the characters *yu yan*.

Peter's citation of Joel's prophecy in Acts 2.17-18 includes the phrases, 'Your sons and daughters will prophesy' and 'they will prophesy'. Both verbs in the Greek text are forms of προφητεύω. The *Union Version* again renders these verbs with the characters *shuo yu yan*.

Another significant passage that refers to prophecy is Acts 19.6, 'When Paul placed his hands on them, the Holy Spirit came on them, and they spoke in tongues and prophesied.' The Greek term translated 'prophesied' is again the verb προφητεύω. The *Union Version* at this point translates with *yu yan*, but adds a note in the margin: 'or "and preached the word" (*jiang dao*)'.[15]

Additional examples can be adduced from other portions of Scripture as well. Jude 14 declares that Enoch 'prophesised'. The Greek term προφητεύω is again rendered in the *Union Version* with the phrase *yu yan*. In Rev. 10.11 John is told that he must 'prophesy.' Here again προφητεύω is translated with *shuo yu yan* in the *Union Version*.

This brief sampling of texts illustrates how the *Union Version* generally translates the verb προφητεύω ('to prophesy') with the Chinese characters *shuo yu yan* or sometimes simply *yu yan*. Indeed, a close analysis reveals that all of the texts that clearly refer to predictive prophecy in the New Testament are translated in this manner.[16] However, it should also be noted that some passages that cannot be confined simply to predictive prophecy are also translated with *yu yan*.[17] Acts 2.17-18 and 19.6 are especially illuminating. Here references to prophecy that almost undoubtedly include the broader activity of 'declaring the wonders of God' (Acts 2.11; also compare 19.6 with 10.46) and not simply predictive prophecy are translated with these characters.

---

[15] 讲道。
[16] These texts include Mt. 11.13, 15.7, Mk 7.6, 14.65, Lk. 1.67, Jn 11.51, 1 Pet. 1.10, Jude 14, Rev. 10.11.
[17] See Acts 2.17, 18, 19.6, and 21.9.

In spite of this general tendency, the *Union Version* does not translate προφητεύω in a uniform manner. A number of references to prophecy in 1 Corinthians are translated with phrases which denote preaching, such as *jiang dao* ('to preach') or *zuo xian zhi jiang dao*[18] ('to engage in prophetic preaching').[19] For example, in 1 Cor. 11.4 Paul writes, 'For every man who prays or prophesies with his head covered dishonors his head.' The term 'prophesies' is a translation of a form of the verb προφητεύω. The *Union Version* translates προφητεύω here with *jiang dao* ('to preach'), although it does add a note in the margin, 'to preach' or 'to prophesy'.[20]

In 1 Cor. 14.1-5 Paul uses forms of the verb προφητεύω no less than four times. Paul writes, 'eagerly desire spiritual gifts, especially the gift of prophecy' (14.1). Paul continues, 'But everyone who prophesies speaks to men for their encouragement and comfort' (14.3). He also adds, '... but he who prophesies edifies the church' (14.4). Thus, Paul concludes, 'I would rather have you prophesy' (14.5). In each instance, the *Union Version* translates with the phrase *zuo xian zhi jiang dao* ('to preach prophetically'). Again, a note is also placed in the margin, 'The original text reads "to prophesy"'.[21]

This pattern continues in 1 Cor. 14.39[22] where Paul writes, 'Therefore, my brothers, be eager to prophesy ....' Here again the *Union Version* translates προφητεύω with the phrase, *zuo xian zhi jiang dao* ('to preach prophetically').

Another interesting example of the *Union Version*'s tendency to refer to preaching rather than prophecy is found in Mt. 7.22. The text reads: 'Many will say to me on that day, 'Lord, Lord, did we not prophesy in your name ....' Although here the Greek text employs the verb προφητεύω, the *Union Version* translates with a phrase that again speaks of proclamation, *chuan dao*.[23]

---

[18] 做先知讲道。
[19] Twelve references to προφητεύω are translated with terms associated with preaching: – *jiang dao* ('to preach'): 1 Cor. 11.4, 5, 13.9, 14.1, 3, 4, 5, 24, 31, 39; *chuan dao* ('to proclaim'): Mt. 7.22 and Rev. 11.3.
[20] '讲道'或作'说预言'。
[21] 原文作'是说预言'。
[22] See also 1 Cor. 12.10, 13.8-9 (2x), 14.22, 24, 29, 31, 39 for the same pattern.
[23] 传道。

The *Union Version* Translation of προφητεύω

Clearly Predictive	Clearly Not Predictive	Ambiguous
Mt. 11.13 (*yu yan*)	Mt. 26.68 (*gao su*)	Mt. 7.22 (*chuan dao*)
Mt. 15.7 (*yu yan*)	Lk 22.64 (*gao su*)	Acts 2.17 (*yu yan*)
Mk 7.6 (*yu yan*)		Acts 2.18 (*yu yan*)
Mk 14.65 (*yu yan*)		Acts 19.6 (*yu yan*)
Lk 1.67 (*yu yan*)		Acts 21.9 (*yu yan*)
Jn 11.51 (*yu yan*)		1 Cor. 11.4 (*jiang dao*)
1 Pet. 1.10 (*yu yan*)		1 Cor. 11.5 (*jiang dao*)
Jude 14 (*yu yan*)		1 Cor. 13.9 (*jiang dao*)
Rev. 10.11 (*yu yan*)		1 Cor. 14.1 (*jiang dao*)
		1 Cor. 14.3 (*jiang dao*)
		1 Cor. 14.4 (*jiang dao*)
	Note:	1 Cor. 14.5 (*jiang dao*)
	yu yan: 'to prophesy'	1 Cor. 14.24 (*jiang dao*)
	gao su: 'to tell'	1 Cor. 14.31 (*jiang dao*)
	chuan dao: 'to proclaim'	1 Cor. 14.39 (*jiang dao*)
	jiang dao: 'to preach'	Rev. 11.3 (*chuan dao*)

These examples illustrate a striking feature of the *Union Version*. When predictive prophecy is clearly in view, often references to Old Testament prophecy or prophecies regarding Jesus, the *Union Version* translates the verb προφητεύω ('to prophesy') with the phrase *yu yan* ('to prophesy') or *shuo yu yan* ('to utter a prophecy'). However, when προφητεύω is used with reference to prophetic utterances in the early church that are not clearly predictive, particularly in 1 Corinthians – texts that might have a bearing on the practice of the contemporary church – the verb is generally translated with phrases associated with preaching, such as *zuo xian zhi jiang dao* ('to preach prophetically'). This lack of uniformity is all the more striking when we remember the principles that guided the translation project. As much as possible, the translators were to 'translate Greek … words occurring in different places and used in the same sense by the same Chinese words' (see Principle

#4 above).[24] Additionally, the translators were to make every effort 'to render literally words and phrases which have a theological or ethical importance' (see Principle #11 above). The translators of the *Union Version* clearly violated these principles when it came to their treatment of prophecy and related terms in the New Testament.[25]

Of course one might argue that the different contexts of the verb προφητεύω justified the different translations employed. Texts in contexts that indicated a predictive prophecy was in view needed to be handled differently from those which seemed to indicate a word of exhortation or encouragement without any predictive element. Yet, given the fact that prophecy in the early church was a rather broad phenomenon, involving both foretelling (e.g. Acts 21.10-11) and words of exhortation (e.g. 1 Cor. 14.3), can these neat distinctions really be made? Is it really possible, for example, to discount a predictive element in the prophetic gift that Paul encourages the believers at Corinth eagerly to desire (1 Cor. 14.1, 39)? Can we limit the impact of the prophetic gift granted at Pentecost (Acts 2.17-18) to predictions concerning future events? It would appear that such judgments are spurious. At the very least, the theologically significant nature of these judgments should have encouraged the translators to opt for a more consistent and literal rendering of the text. The fact that they did not indicates that another agenda was at work.

Additionally, it appears that the translators of the *Union Version* missed another important matter. Even references to prophecy as a non-predictive word of exhortation or encouragement are not adequately translated with terms associated with preaching. This is the case because prophecy in the New Testament, even as a non-predictive word of exhortation, is normally portrayed as a spontaneous, Spirit-inspired message directed to the specific needs of a community, a message that is neither pre-planned nor primarily

---

[24] Principle #3 essentially reaffirms this point, but in a slightly different way, 'Passages expressed in the same terms and in the same or similar connection in the original, translate in the uniform manner' (see the reference above).

[25] Although it should be noted that they did on occasion put alternative translations in the margin in accordance with Principle #15: 'When two or more interpretations seem quite or nearly equally good, give one in the text and the other, or others, in the margin' (see the reference above).

the product of prior preparation or study.[26] Thus, the semantic range of terms associated with preaching is simply too narrow to do προφητεύω justice. The essential concept conveyed with these terms – a pre-planned message that is the result of prior study of the Scriptures – is, in the final analysis, misleading.[27]

Some might question whether the difference between the Chinese phrases *shou yu yan* ('to prophesy') and *zuo xian zhi jiang dao* ('to preach prophetically') is as significant as I suggest. I believe the following personal experience sheds light on this question. Earlier this year (2005) I asked four Chinese church leaders what *shuo yu yan* and *zuo xian zhi jiang dao* meant? They emphasized that these two terms did not have the same meaning. They indicated that *shuo yu yan* had to do with speaking a word from the Lord for the church with reference either to the present or the future. They stressed that this was not presenting biblical teaching, but rather a more immediate, direct word for a specific situation. They understood the phrase to refer to a spontaneous, unplanned message inspired by the Holy Spirit that brings encouragement or direction to the church.

On the other hand, in their understanding *zuo xian zhi jiang dao* refers to preaching. This phrase speaks of presenting biblical truth – that is, truth that has been gleaned from the study of Scripture – to the church. When I asked how this differed from preaching (*jiang dao*), they answered that it is essentially the same.

As we continued to speak of the value and dangers of prophecy, they told the following story. At their church's Bible school (in 1999), a group of church leaders and faculty members gathered

---

[26] See especially 1 Cor. 14.29-33, Eph. 4.11, and 1 Tim. 4.14. Gordon Fee, on the basis of the evidence in 1 Corinthians 14, states that prophecy 'consisted of spontaneous, Spirit-inspired, intelligible messages, orally delivered in the gathered assembly, intended for the edification or encouragement of the people.' And he continues in an attached footnote, 'Thus it is *not* the delivery of a previously prepared sermon' (italics his). See Gordon D. Fee, *The First Epistle to the Corinthians* (NICNT; Grand Rapids: Wm. B. Eerdmans Publishing Company, 1987), p. 595 and p. 595, n. 73.

[27] The leading contemporary New Testament scholars writing in this field agree that New Testament prophecy cannot be equated with preaching. See James D.G. Dunn, *Jesus and the Spirit: A Study of the Religious and Charismatic Experience of Jesus and the First Christians as Reflected in the New Testament* (London: SCM Press, 1975), pp. 228-29, Fee, *The First Epistle to the Corinthians*, p. 595, n. 73, and Max Turner, *The Holy Spirit and Spiritual Gifts Then and Now* (Carlisle: Paternoster Press, 1996), pp. 206-12.

together for a prayer meeting. They were all very discouraged –
they had faced a lot of opposition – and they did not feel like
praying. They were tired, discouraged, and did not even feel able
to pray. In the midst of this setting, Lu Xiaomin, the famous
songwriter, stood up and began to sing a song, *zhan shi, zhan shi, qi
lai* ('soldiers, soldiers, stand up'). As the words of the song rang
out through the room, they all felt the encouragement and
strength of the Lord. It was evident that this song was exactly
what they needed to hear. My friends spoke of this as a wonderful
illustration of the Holy Spirit breaking in and, in an unanticipated
and unplanned manner, inspiring a sister to bring much-needed
encouragement to the group. They felt this was a good example
of prophecy (*yu yan*) edifying the church.

We have examined the manner in which the translators of the
Union Version translated the verb 'to prophesy' (προφητεύω) and
we have found, on the one hand, a striking inconsistency, and on
the other, a clear tendency. The inconsistency is found in the fact
that the *Union Version* uses different terms to translate the same
verb. The tendency is seen in the translators' predilection for describing prophecy in the early church, especially in settings like 1
Corinthians 14 which might have a bearing on contemporary practice, as the presentation of biblical truth gleaned from the study
of Scripture (i.e. preaching). We have noted that this method of
translation is reductionistic: predictive prophecy is arbitrarily ruled
out in some cases. Furthermore, this translation is misleading: the
semantic range of prophecy, which includes spontaneous, Spirit-
inspired utterances, is quite different from that of terms associated with preaching. We are now in a position to examine the possible reasons for this unfortunate tendency on the part of the
translators of the *Union Version*. Why did they tend to identify
prophecy with preaching?

The Presuppositions Behind the Translation

As we begin our inquiry into the possible reasons for the unique
manner in which the translators of the *Union Version* translated
προφητεύω, it might be helpful first to note factors that should be
ruled out. Two in particular come to mind. First, we have noted
that the translators of the *Union Version* New Testament were in-

structed by the Protestant Missionary Conference of 1890 to base their translation on the *Revised English Version* (Oxford, 1881) and its underlying Greek text. Is it not possible that the *Union Version's* idiosyncratic translation of προφητεύω actually stems from this text? Were the *Union Version* translators simply following the example of the translators of the *Revised English Version* as they translated the verb 'to prophesy'? As plausible as this rationale may seem, careful examination of the *Revised English Version* reveals that these questions must be answered in the negative. Unlike the Chinese *Union Version*, the *Revised English Version* consistently translates the verb προφητεύω with the verb 'to prophesy.' So, for example, the *Revised English Version* of 1 Cor. 14.1 reads as follows, 'Follow after love: yet desire earnestly spiritual gifts, but rather that ye may prophesy.'[28] Clearly, the underlying text employed by the translators cannot be blamed for the peculiarities of the *Union Version* at this point.

Secondly, although it might be tempting to suggest that the translators were consciously reacting to the emergence of the modern Pentecostal movement, this is extremely unlikely. The *Union Version* New Testament was first published in 1907, the same year the first Pentecostal missionaries impacted by the Azusa Street revival arrived in Hong Kong.[29] While it is true that this initial translation of the New Testament was revised and published together with the translation of the Old Testament in 1919, producing the *Union Version* that we know today, it is unlikely that the revisions of the 1907 version impacted the key texts we have examined in any significant way. I am writing from China and do not have access to the 1907 *Union Version* translation, so I am unable to speak on this matter authoritatively. If it could be shown that the translation tendencies noted above were introduced into the text after 1907, then a case could be made that the translators were indeed consciously reacting to the emerging Pentecostal movement. However, as I have noted, I believe this to be highly

---

[28] *The New Testament of Our Lord and Saviour Jesus Christ, Translated out of the Greek: being the version set forth A.D. 1611 compared with the most ancient authorities and revised, A.D. 1881* (Oxford: Oxford University Press, 1881).

[29] See Luke Wesley, *The Church in China: Persecuted, Pentecostal, and Powerful* (AJPSS 2; Baguio City, Philippines: AJPS Books, 2004), pp. 54-57.

unlikely. The translators produced most of their work prior to any encounter with Pentecostal believers.

Rather, I believe the evidence suggests that the translators were driven in their decisions at this point by unconscious theological assumptions. They were products of their era, greatly impacted by their own theological tradition, and this, I would argue, was the decisive factor shaping their particular approach to the translation task. We have already noted that the three key translators – C.W. Mateer (Presbyterian), Chauncey Goodrich (Congregationalist), and F.W. Baller (Baptist) – were all steeped in the Reformed tradition. As such, they would have been very much aware of John Calvin's teaching on prophecy. Calvin's influence, either directly or indirectly, undoubtedly would have been great. It is precisely here where we find the key reason behind the translation tendency outlined above.

Martin Luther and John Calvin were of one mind when it came to prophecy. Luther was not happy with what he perceived to be the subjective excesses of prophets, whether they were attached to the Roman church or the radical wing of the Protestant Reformation. So Luther sought to root prophecy in the objective ground of the Word of God. He wrote, 'When Paul or the other apostles interpreted the Old Testament, their interpretation was prophecy *(On Joel 2.28)*.'[30] For Luther, prophets were those 'who can expound the Scriptures and ably interpret and teach the difficult books.'[31]

John Calvin's position on prophecy was similar to that of Luther. He too felt the need to curb the abuses of subjective revelation. Calvin thus viewed the canon as the ultimate and final revelation to the church. Any ongoing prophetic activity was limited to a further explication of this word.[32] Calvin, for example, in his discussion of 1 Thess. 5.20 understands 'prophesying to mean the

---

[30] I am indebted to C.M. Robeck for this reference. See C.M. Robeck, 'Gift of Prophecy', *The New International Dictionary of Pentecostal Charismatic Movements*, Stanley M. Burgess and Eduard M van der Maas, eds. (revised and expanded; Grand Rapids: Zondervan, 2002), pp. 999-1012; quotation from p. 1010.

[31] Robeck, 'Gift of Prophecy', p. 1010. Robeck cites the preface of Luther's *On Zechariah* as the source for this quotation.

[32] Robeck, 'Gift of Prophecy', p. 1010.

interpretation of Scripture applied to present need.'[33] Further-more, in his *Commentary on Romans* (12.5) Calvin wrote, 'Proph-ecy ... is simply the right understanding of scripture and the par-ticular gift of expounding it.'[34] C.M. Robeck notes that Calvin's 'emphasis was placed on the prophetic as something that did not occur spontaneously ... It did not seem to be fresh revelation but primarily correct understanding and application of existing revela-tion.'[35] In short, Calvin understood prophecy to be essentially preaching.

The connection, then, between Calvin's perspective on proph-ecy and the translation tendency outlined above is apparent. It is evident that the translators of the *Union Version* New Testament simply reflected their own theological tradition's perception of prophecy as they went about translating the biblical text. In this way, Calvin's understanding of prophecy as preaching became en-shrined in the Chinese New Testament.

It should be noted that this approach to translating the verb 'to prophesy' (προφητεύω) is not unique to the Chinese *Union Ver-sion*. The *Today's English Version* (*TEV*) of the New Testament rep-resents a striking parallel.[36] For example, the *TEV* translates Jesus' words in Matthew 15.7 as, 'You hypocrites! How right Isaiah was when he prophesied about you!' Yet the same verb employed here is translated rather differently in 1 Cor. 14.1, 'Set your hearts on spiritual gifts, especially the gift of proclaiming God's message'. This theologically loaded translation is, we have suggested, inaccu-rate and misleading. It is driven by concerns to protect the author-ity of the canon of Scripture – concerns which contemporary scholars from the Reformed tradition have acknowledged are without foundation[37] – and it flies in the face of contemporary

---

[33] This quotation from Calvin is cited in Dunn, *Jesus and the Spirit*, p. 418, n. 147.

[34] Robeck, 'The Gift of Prophecy', p. 1010.

[35] Robeck, 'The Gift of Prophecy', p. 1010.

[36] The quotations attributed to the *TEV* which follow are from the *Good News New Testament: The New Testament in Today's English Version, fourth edition* (New York: American Bible Society, 1976).

[37] More recent scholarship has emphasized that Paul 'relativizes the author-ity of prophetic communications in the church' (quote from Turner, *The Holy Spirit and Spiritual Gifts Now and Then*, p. 217). Thus, prophecy need not be viewed as threatening the authority of the Scriptures. See Wayne Grudem, *The*

New Testament scholarship on the nature of prophecy.[38] Nevertheless, given the wide range of translations available in the English language, an idiosyncratic translation like this translation is not so problematic. English speakers generally have access to many translations and may choose and compare as they please.

The situation in China, however, is very different. As we have noted, most Chinese believers have access to only one translation of the Bible. For these believers, the *Union Version* represents the only means available to them to read or hear the written Word of God. Additionally, the availability of other Christian books – books that might provide the perspective needed to deal with issues such as this – is extremely limited. The implications, then, of an inaccurate or misleading translation in the *Union Version* are thus magnified.[39]

It is difficult to know how one should respond to this situation since it is hard to imagine the acceptance of another translation in China in the foreseeable future. However, a short-term response might include the production of study materials that provide teaching on this topic in a sensitive manner. A more far-sighted response would include encouraging Chinese Christians to produce modern translations of the Bible that show an awareness of and sensitivity to the issues outlined above.[40]

Gift of Prophecy in 1 Corinthians (Washington: UPA, 1982), Turner, *The Holy Spirit and Spiritual Gifts Then and Now,* pp. 213-17, and Sam Storms, *The Beginner's Guide to Spiritual Gifts* (Ann Arbor, MI: Servant Publications, 2002), pp. 85-118.

[38] See Dunn, *Jesus and the Spirit,* Fee, *The First Epistle to the Corinthians,* Grudem, *The Gift of Prophecy in 1 Corinthians,* and Turner, *The Holy Spirit and Spiritual Gifts Then and Now,* as cited above.

[39] Other texts in the Chinese *Union Version* that might reflect 'anti-charismatic bias' or, at the very least, appear to reflect inappropriate and overly rationalistic translations include a group of texts where probable references to the Spirit of God are translated as references to the human spirit or attitudes. For example, in Acts 20.22 Paul is 'compelled by the Holy Spirit' (δεδεμένος ἐγὼ τῷ πνεύματι) to go to Jerusalem. The *Union Version* translates this phrase as 'Paul felt deeply compelled' (*xin shen po qie*). See also Jn 4.23, Rom. 7.6, 8.15, 1 Cor. 14.2, 2 Cor. 3.6, 12.19, Phil. 1.27, 2.2.

[40] Several modern Chinese translations of the New Testament have been produced. As we have noted, none of these have been widely accepted in China. Additionally, all these translations (at least all that I am aware of) follow the *Union Version* and translate the verb 'to prophesy' in 1 Corinthians with terms associated with preaching, such as *jiang dao*. For example, *The Contemporary Gospel – Chinese Living New Testament* (*dang dai fu yin*), published in 1981, translates 1 Cor. 14.1 with, '… especially the gift of prophetic preaching' (*zuo xian*

Conclusion

Our analysis has revealed that the translators of the Chinese *Union Version* New Testament deviated from their guiding principles when they translated the verb 'to prophesy' (προφητεύω). They did not translate the verb consistently nor did they render literally this verb with obvious theological significance. Rather, they translated the verb in light of the prevailing attitudes toward prophecy current in their own Reformed tradition. Thus, the *Union Version* translators translate references to, in their estimation, predictive prophecy – generally references to Old Testament prophecy or prophecies regarding Jesus – with the phrase *yu yan* ('to prophesy') or *shuo yu yan* ('to utter a prophecy'). Yet they translate references to prophetic utterances in the early church not perceived to be predictive, particularly those texts in 1 Corinthians that might have a bearing on the practice of the contemporary church, with phrases associated with preaching, such as *zuo xian zhi jiang dao* ('to preach prophetically'). We have argued that this tendency to identify prophecy with preaching is both reductionistic and misleading. It is reductionistic in that predictive prophecy is arbitrarily and inappropriately dismissed as a valid dimension of the semantic range of the verb προφητεύω in many instances. Furthermore, this tendency is misleading because the semantic range of prophecy, which includes spontaneous, Spirit-inspired utterances, is quite different from that of terms associated with preaching. In short, the translators of the *Union Version* have unconsciously foisted Calvin's view of prophecy as preaching onto the biblical text.

Since the Chinese *Union Version* is used by virtually all of the Christians in China and attempts to use other, more modern translations are viewed with great suspicion, this idiosyncratic element of the *Union Version* is especially problematic. It is hoped that this study might stimulate further discussion on this topic and encourage future translators of the Chinese New Testament to

---

zhi jiang dao de en ci). *The New Chinese Version Bible* (*xin yi ben*), published in 2002, offers essentially the same translation. The *Today's Chinese Version* (*xian dai zhong wen yi ben*), which is based on the *Today's English Version*, renders 1 Cor. 14.1 with, '… especially the gift of proclaiming God's message' (*xuan jiang shang di xin xi de en ci*).

deal with this matter in a manner more faithful to the intended meaning of the biblical text.

2

THE DIVINE SPIRIT OR THE HUMAN SPIRIT?

Not long ago I had one of those epiphany moments. A moment when, in a flash, previous perceptions are challenged and a new paradigm, a new way of looking at a particular issue, comes into focus. It happened during a beautiful evening in May some years ago. Earlier that day I had presented a lecture for the Yong San Theological Symposium in Seoul, Korea. Then, for the evening meal, the presenters gathered together around a large table with Dr. David Yonggi Cho and his wife. Dr. Cho began to reminisce about the early days of his ministry and how, often through visions, the Lord had encouraged him to move forward in risky and surprising ways. In preparation for the symposium, I had read a number of Dr. Cho's works. In his writings, Dr. Cho often highlights the importance of being led by the Spirit and spiritual vision. That evening, as Dr. Cho was sharing one particularly inspiring story, I was drawn to the term 'vision'. As he spoke, the words of Acts 2.17 came to mind: 'Your young men will see visions, your old men will dream dreams.' Of course, I knew the passage well. It was like an old friend. I had spent the better part of four years studying this and related passages in Luke–Acts during my PhD studies. And yet, in that moment, I knew that I had missed something – something very important.

'Visions' and Supernatural Guidance: A Lukan Theme

As the text of Acts 2.17-21 raced through my mind, I considered it again:

[v. 17] *In the last days, God says,* [Joel: 'after these things']
I will pour out my Spirit on all people.
Your sons and daughters will prophesy
Your young men will see visions, [Joel: these lines are inverted]
Your old men will dream dreams.

[v. 18] *Even* on *my* servants, both men and women, [additions to
Joel]
I will pour out my Spirit in those days,
And they will prophesy.

[v. 19] I will show wonders in the heaven *above*
And *signs* on the earth *below,*
Blood and fire and billows of smoke.

[v. 20] The sun will be turned to darkness and the moon to
blood
Before the coming of the great and glorious day of the Lord.

[v. 21] And everyone who calls on the name of the Lord will be
saved.
(Acts 2.17-21; modification of Joel 2.28-32 italicized).

Ever since my days of study at the University of Aberdeen, I
had recognized that Luke carefully shapes this quotation from the
LXX in order to highlight important theological themes and
truths. Three modifications are particularly striking:

First, Luke inserts the phrase, 'And they will prophesy', into the
quotation in v. 18. It is as if Luke is saying, 'whatever you do,
don't miss this!' In these last days the servants of God will be
anointed by the Spirit to proclaim his good news. They will
prophesy! This is what is *now* taking place. Of course, this theme
of Spirit-inspired witness runs throughout the narrative of Acts. I
was aware of all this.

Secondly, with the addition of a few words in v. 19, Luke transforms Joel's text to read: 'I will show wonders in the heaven *above*,
and *signs* on the earth *below*'. In this way, Luke consciously links the

miracles associated with Jesus (notice the very first verse that follows the quotation from Joel: 'Jesus ... was a man accredited by God to you by miracles, wonders and signs', Acts 2.22) and the early church (e.g. 2.43) together with the cosmic portents listed by Joel (Acts 2.19-20). All are 'signs and wonders' that mark the end of the age. For Luke, 'these last days' – that period inaugurated with Jesus' birth and leading up to the Day of the Lord – represents an epoch marked by 'signs and wonders'. Luke, then, is not only conscious of the significant role that miracles have played in the growth of the early church, he also anticipates that these 'signs and wonders' will continue to characterize the ministry of the church in our day ('these last days'). Again, I was aware of all of this.

However, there is one other alteration that I began to reconsider. In v. 17 Luke alters the order of the two lines that refer to young men having visions and old men dreaming dreams. In Joel, the old men dreaming dreams comes first. But Luke reverses the order: 'Your young men will see visions, your old men will dream dreams' (Acts 2.17). In my earlier days of study, I had noted this modification of Joel's text. However, I did not feel that this reflected any significant theological or literary motive. I felt that it was purely stylistic. Perhaps Luke simply wanted to go chronologically, moving from young men to old men. It really wasn't clear why this change was made, but it didn't amount to much. That was my thinking and that is what I wrote.[1]

Yet, in that moment in Korea, as I listened to Dr. Cho speak of visions and divine direction, the thought came to me. I don't know why I hadn't thought of this earlier. It's actually a bit embarrassing to reveal how slow I was to pick up on this point. But the thought came to me (20 years later, but it came none the less): visions play a huge role in the story of Acts! God uses visions to guide the church at key, pivotal points in its mission. What about dreams? Dreams are not so prominent in Luke's narrative. Perhaps Luke's alteration here serves to highlight what he thought most important, a theme that would recur throughout his story:

---

[1] See Menzies, *The Development of Early Christian Pneumatology with special reference to Luke–Acts* (JSNTSup 54; Sheffield: JSOT Press, 1991), p. 218.

the Lord delights to speak to us. The Lord will direct his church, and he often does it through visions! A survey of Acts reveals, I would suggest, that this alteration is not simply an insignificant stylistic change. (I was wrong to draw this conclusion in my previous writings). No, this is not merely a whim or slip of the eye. On the contrary, this subtle shift is intentional. Luke gives the reference to 'visions' pride of place in order to emphasize its importance. With this modification of the LXX, Luke highlights a theme that he sees as vitally important and which recurs throughout his narrative.

A survey of the key terms is instructive. First, we find that the terms associated with dreams and dreaming occur only here in the book of Acts. The term translated 'shall dream' is a future passive of ἐνυπνιάζω. This verb occurs only here and in Jude 8 in the entire New Testament. The noun, ἐνύπνιον ('dream'), is found nowhere else in Acts or the rest of the New Testament. Clearly, Luke is not big on dreaming.[2]

Luke, however, loves to recount stories that reference guidance through 'visions'. At first glance this may not appear to be the case. The noun translated 'visions' in v. 17, ὅρασις, occurs four times in the New Testament and only here in Acts. The other three occurrences are all found in Revelation. But appearances are often misleading and this is the case here. Luke uses another term, a close cousin to ὅρασις, the neuter noun, ὅραμα, often and at decisive points in his narrative to refer to 'visions'. The noun ὅραμα occurs 12 times in the New Testament and 11 of these occurrences are found in the book of Acts.[3] Luke is, indeed, fond of visions. Although in Acts 2.17 Luke retains the language of the LXX, elsewhere in his narrative he employs his preferred, very similar term, to speak of 'visions'.

As I have noted, references to visions are not only plentiful in Luke's narrative, they also come at strategic moments. Paul's ministry is launched by means of a divine encounter brought about by visions. Ananias is led to Paul by means of a vision (Acts 9.10). In this vision Ananias is told that Paul has also received a vision, re-

---

[2] Note how Luke describes revelatory experiences at night, which might have taken place during sleep, as 'visions' and not 'dreams' (e.g. Acts 16.9-10).

[3] Acts 7.31; 9.10, 12; 10: 3, 17, 19; 11.5; 12.9; 16.9, 10; 18.9; and then also in Mt. 17.9.

vealing to him that Ananias will come and pray for the restoration of Paul's sight (Acts 9.12). Of course, all of this transpires. Paul is healed, filled with the Spirit, and begins to preach with great boldness that Jesus is the Son of God.

The pivotal event recorded in Acts 10, the conversion of Cornelius and his household through the preaching of Peter, is also facilitated through visions. The narrative begins with a description of Cornelius' vision, which directs Cornelius to seek out Peter (Acts 10.3). Just as Cornelius' emissaries arrive, Peter too has a vision (Acts 10.17, 19; 11.5). This vision prepares Peter's heart for the ministry that God has in store for him. Peter, directed by the vision, will be an agent through which God shatters barriers of prejudice and hatred, and the early church, at this point still entirely Jewish, will begin to embrace Gentiles.

During Paul's second missionary journey, just as it appears that Paul is hopelessly lost and doesn't know where to go, he receives his Macedonian vision (Acts 16.9, 10). This vision represents a significant turning point in Paul's ministry. In the face of great opposition, strong churches are planted in Philippi, Thessalonica, Berea, and Corinth. In Corinth, in the midst of hostility and abuse, in a vision Paul is encouraged to remain there and to keep on preaching, for, he is told, 'no one is going to attack and harm you, because I have many people in this city' (Acts 18.9-10).

Certainly the Lord uses other means to direct his followers as they seek to proclaim the gospel. For example, Philip is directed to the Ethiopian eunuch by an angel (Acts 8.26) and by the leading of the Holy Spirit (8.29). So, visions are not the only means that God uses to guide his church. Yet Luke's point seems to be very clear. The early church was led in remarkable ways by visions and special instances of divine direction. It was led to break through barriers of fear and prejudice. Oh, how we need this today! Oh, how we need to be sensitive to his leading, so that our fears and our prejudices might be shattered. But the really powerful point that Luke makes is this: God delights to do precisely this *for us*. Just as he led them (the apostolic church), so also he will lead us. He will guide us in very personal, special ways, if we are open and listening. The crucial point that cannot be missed is this: By linking the 'visions' of Joel's prophecy (Acts 2.17) with the visions of the early church, Luke is in effect saying that in 'these last days' (remember Luke's church and ours is rooted firmly in this period) the mission of the church must be directed by God, who will lead his end-time prophets in special ways, including visions, angelic visitations, and the prompting of the Spirit, so that we might fulfill our calling to take the gospel to 'the ends of the earth.' In short, for Luke, the experience of the early church, a church that is supernaturally led by God, serves as a model for our church and for our mission.

The *Union Version's* Rationalistic Bias: An Examination of Specific Texts

Luke's call for an openness to God's special leading – a sense of expectancy that God will guide us in very special and personal ways, even through visions, angelic visitations, and the leading of the Spirit – has not been readily received by many Protestants. Unfortunately, this rationalistic bias has exerted considerable influence on the translators of the Chinese *Union Version* of the New Testament. In the previous chapter I argued that the translators of the *Union Version* unconsciously foisted Calvin's view of prophecy as preaching onto the biblical text. I would now like to look briefly at another peculiarity of the *Union Version* translation of the New Testament. I refer to the translators' tendency to translate references to the Spirit of God as references to the human spirit or human attitudes. This tendency is consistent with the *Union Version* translators' treatment of prophecy as described above, in that it also serves to downplay humankind's ability to hear God's voice in an immediate and subjective manner apart from the study of Scripture. Specifically, we shall examine how the *Union Version* translators translate selected texts that contain the Greek term, πνεῦμα ('spirit' or 'Spirit').

Acts 20.22 & 19.21
We begin our examination with a look at Acts 20.22, where we read that Paul is 'compelled by the Spirit' (δεδεμένος ἐγὼ τῷ πνεύματι) to go to Jerusalem. The *Union Version* translates this phrase as, 'Paul felt deeply compelled' (*xin shen po qie*).[4] Clearly the

---

[4] 心甚迫切。

Union Version translators understand πνεῦμα here to refer to Paul's spirit rather than the Spirit of God. On this reading of the text, Paul is not explicitly directed by the Holy Spirit to go to Jerusalem, rather he 'feels' deeply about this matter. Although this interpretation is grammatically possible and followed by some English translations,[5] it is almost certainly wrong. Luke's tendency throughout his two-volume work to present the Spirit as the driving and directive force behind the mission of Jesus and the church as well as the immediate context, which highlights the Holy Spirit's role in guiding Paul ('in every city the Holy Spirit warns me ...', Acts 20.23), speak decisively against it.

This judgment is confirmed by Acts 19.21, which is the earliest reference to Paul's compulsion to go to Jerusalem. Here, Paul 'resolves in the Spirit (ἐν τῷ πνεύματι) ... to go to Jersualem'. (Acts 19.21).[6] Again, the *Union Version* translates the reference to πνεῦμα as referring to Paul's state of mind: 'Paul determined in his heart' (*bao luo xinli ding yi*)[7] to go to Jerusalem (Acts 19.21).[8] Yet this verse goes on to quote Paul's declaration that his trip is based on much more than a personal plan. Paul declares, 'I must visit Rome also' (Acts 19.21). The term δεῖ, which refers to the necessity of an action or event, is used here. In Acts, Luke frequently uses this term to refer to divinely ordained happenings. Martin Mittlestadt correctly notes, 'the fact that δεῖ is used as part of [Paul's] proposed travel itinerary lends itself in favor of a purpose which is divinely inspired'.[9] A future use of δεῖ also occurs at Acts 23.11 (as well as 27.24, 26) where Paul receives assurance from 'the Lord that his journey is indeed under sovereign direction'.[10] Mittlestadt aptly concludes that Luke would hardly suggest that

---

[5] See, for example, the New American Standard Bible. Note also Eugene Peterson's translation in *The Message*, which has Paul declare, 'I feel compelled to go to Jerusalem' (Acts 20.22 in *The Message: The Bible in Contemporary Language*, translated by Eugene H. Peterson [Colorado Springs: NavPress, 2002]).

[6] I am following Marty Mittlestadt's fine work and translation at this point. See Martin Mittlestadt, *The Spirit and Suffering in Luke–Acts: Implications for a Pentecostal Pneumatology* (JPTSup 26; London: T&T Clark International, 2004), p. 122.

[7] 保罗心里定意。

[8] Peterson, in *The Message*, translates similarly: 'Paul *decided* it was time to move on to ... Jersualem' (italics mine). See also the NIV, 'Paul decided ...' (Acts 19.21).

[9] Mittlestadt, *Suffering and the Spirit*, pp. 122-23.

[10] Mittlestadt, *Suffering and the Spirit*, pp. 123.

the trip to Jerusalem and Rome, which is clearly described as a divine necessity in Acts 23.11, began purely as a human intention. Indeed, throughout his journeys in Acts, Paul's course is directed by the Spirit of God (Acts 13.1-4; 14.26; 16.6-10).[11] It is safe to say, then, that the occurrences of πνεῦμα in Acts 20.22 and 19.21 refer to the Holy Spirit leading Paul, not merely to Paul's own personal convictions or feelings.

Acts 18.25

In Acts 18.24-28 we are introduced to the intriguing and passionate man named, Apollos. In v. 25 Apollos is described as one who spoke zealously in the Spirit/his spirit (ζέων τῷ πνεύματι). The NIV understands πνεῦμα here to refer to the human spirit and thus translates, 'he [Apollos] spoke with great fervor' (Acts 18.25).[12] The *Union Version* also takes this phrase, ζέων τῷ πνεύματι, as a description of Apollos' passionate and fiery nature and renders the phrase in a similar manner, *xinli huo re* (literally, he spoke as if 'his heart was burning').[13]

Although this line of interpretation and the resulting translation is possible, again I doubt if it really captures Luke's intent. This translation not only fails to account for Luke's unique emphasis on Spirit-empowered speech, an emphasis that runs throughout his two-volume work,[14] it also appears to be based on the faulty notion that somehow, in Luke's eyes, Apollos and his Ephesian converts were not truly Christians.

The crucial question centers on the status of the Ephesian disciples, who are described as not having received the gift of the Spirit (19.1): Are they truly disciples of Jesus? When the immediate context, which contains the closely related pericope concerning Apollos (Acts 18.24-28), is considered, the evidence demands an affirmative response. Apollos' standing can hardly be questioned, for Luke indicates that, 'he had been instructed in the way of the Lord' and 'taught about Jesus accurately' (18.25). The latter

---

[11] Mittlestadt, *Suffering and the Spirit*, pp. 123.

[12] Numerous other English translations follow this pattern, including the New American Bible, the Revised English Bible, the New Revised Standard Version, and the New Jerusalem Bible.

[13] 心里火热。

[14] See, for example, Luke 1.41-42, 67; 2.27-28; 4.18; 10.21; 12.11-12; Acts 4.13, 31; 5.32; 6.10 9.31: 13.9, 52.

phrase, descriptive of Paul's preaching in 28.31, suggests that Apollos preached the Christian gospel. Since according to Luke the gift of the Spirit is not inextricably bound to the rite of baptism (e.g. Acts 8.17; 10.44), there is no contradiction in his portrait of Apollos as an articulate and anointed minister of the gospel who had not received Christian baptism. Similarly, Apollos' charismatic experience does not presuppose an awareness of the Pentecostal event or promise. Our experience often precedes our ability to understand or proclaim it.

It is also important to note that Apollos' lack of understanding with regard to Christian baptism does not preclude his contact with the Ephesian disciples, who had not heard of the availability of the Spirit. On the contrary, Luke has carefully constructed the narrative in order to emphasize the relationship between Apollos and the Ephesians (cf. 19.1), all of whom knew only 'the baptism of John' (18.25; 19.3). The clear implication is that the twelve from Ephesus were converts of the able preacher active in the same city.[15] We must therefore conclude that in Luke's estimation the Ephesians were, like Apollos, disciples of Jesus. This conclusion is supported by Luke's description of the Ephesians as 'disciples' (μαθηταί; 19.1), for when he employs the term without any further qualification it always refers to disciples of Jesus.[16] And since 'faith' (πίστις) is the essence of discipleship,[17] the description of the Ephesians as 'believers' (19.2) confirms these findings.[18]

All of this suggests that, in Luke's estimation, Apollos was an effective and anointed Christian evangelist. Although Apollos was

---

[15] For the literary connections between 18.24-28 and 19.1-7 see M. Wolter, 'Apollos und die ephesinischen Johannesjünger (Acts 18.24-19.7)', *Zeitschrift für die neutestamentliche Wissenschaft* 78 (1987), pp. 61-62, 71.

[16] See Lk. 9.16, 18, 54; 10.23; 16.1; 17.22; 18.15; 19.29; 19.37; 20.45; 22.39, 45; Acts 6.1, 2, 7; 9.10, 19, 26, 38; 11.26, 29; 13.52; 14.20, 22, 28; 15.10; 16.1; 18.23, 27; 19.1, 9, 30; 20.1, 30; 21.4, 16. K. Haacker, 'Einige Fälle von "erlebter Rede" im Neuen Testament', *Novum Testamentum* 12 (1970), p. 75: 'Der absolut Gebrauch von μαθητής wird von allen Auslegern als eine Bezeichnung für Christen erkannt.'

[17] See K.H. Rengstorf, 'μαθητής', *TDNT*, IV, p. 447.

[18] See for example F.F. Bruce, *Commentary on the Book of Acts* (NICNT; Grand Rapids: Eerdmans, 1984), p. 385: 'Paul's question, "Did ye receive the Holy Spirit when ye believed?" suggests strongly that he regarded them as true believers in Christ'.

deficient in his understanding of the proper mode of Christian baptism, Luke commends him in every other way. Indeed, Apollos played a significant role in the advance of the gospel that Luke so skillfully chronicles. It seems natural that Luke would describe him as one who 'spoke passionately as a result of the Spirit's inspiration.'

1 Corinthians 14.2

Another interesting translation is found in 1 Cor. 14.2, which is rendered in the NIV as follows: 'For anyone who speaks in a tongue does not speak to men, but to God. Indeed, no one understands him; he utters mysteries with his spirit.'[19] Our primary concern here is the translation of the phrase, πνεύματι δὲ λαλεῖ μυστήρια ('he utters mysteries with his spirit'). The *Union Version* also translates the reference to πνεῦμα here as alluding to the human spirit. The mysteries are uttered *zai xinling li*[20] ('in the heart' or 'human spirit'). Again, it is virtually certain that this translation does not accurately convey Paul's intent. As Gordon Fee notes, 1 Cor. 12.7-11 clearly indicates, 'that tongues is the manifestation of the Spirit of God through the human speaker.'[21] Additionally, in Paul's writings πνεῦμα in the dative is generally anarthrous when referring to the Holy Spirit and the opposite is true when referring to the human spirit.[22] Fee draws the appropriate conclusion: 'It does not seem remotely possible that in this context Paul would suddenly refer to speaking "with one's own spirit", rather than by the Holy Spirit.'[23] Here too, then, we find a New Testament text that highlights humankind's capacity to commune with God, for Paul declares that it is through the inspiration of the Holy Spirit that we may utter these divine mysteries.

---

[19] The NIV does add a footnote after 'spirit' which offers 'by the Spirit' as an alternative reading.

[20] 在心灵里.

[21] Gordon D. Fee, *The First Epistle to the Corinthians* (NICNT; Grand Rapids: Eerdmans, 1987), p. 656.

[22] See Fee, *The First Epistle to the Corinthians*, p. 578, n. 43 and Gordon Fee, 'Translational Tendenz: English Versions and Πνεῦμα in Paul' in Graham N. Stanton, Bruce W. Longenecker, and Stephen C. Barton (eds.), *The Holy Spirit and Christian Origins: Essays in Honor of James D.G. Dunn* (Grand Rapids: William B. Eerdmans, 2004), p. 354.

[23] Fee, *The First Epistle to the Corinthians*, p. 656.

2 Corinthians 12.18

In 2 Cor. 12.18 Paul writes, 'Titus did not exploit you, did he? Did we not act in the same spirit (τῷ αὐτῷ πνεύματι) and follow the same course?' The *Union Version*, in a manner similar to the NIV, the KJV, and many other English translations, again opts for translating πνεῦμα here as a reference to the human spirit, rendering the term with the characters *xinling*[24] ('human spirit' or 'inner spirit'). Yet, Fee argues convincingly that this rendering should also be questioned. He notes that in 1 Cor. 12.4-11 Paul speaks of 'the same Spirit' as he begins and ends his discussion. Paul also repeatedly uses the phrases 'by the same Spirit' in 1 Cor. 12.8-10. No one would question that the phrase here refers to the Holy Spirit. Fee concludes that translators 'disregard Paul's own clear usage and opt for a meaning for πνεῦμα that fits the range of meanings for the word "spirit" in English, but for which there is very little, if any, evidence in the Greek world.'[25] The evidence, then, suggests that in 2 Cor. 12.18 Paul, with his rhetorical questions, reminds the Corinthians that both Titus and Paul were inspired and led by the Spirit of God. Unfortunately, the *Union Version* and most English translations do not reflect this fact.

John 4.23

John 4.23 offers another interesting example. The text reads: 'Yet a time is coming and has now come when the true worshippers will worship the Father in spirit and truth [ἐν πνεύματι καὶ ἀληθείᾳ], for they are the kind of worshippers the Father seeks.' The *Union Version*, like the NIV, interprets this occurrence of πνεῦμα as a reference to the human spirit. Again, the characters *xinling*[26] (lit., 'heart-spirit') are employed to translate the text. Although there is a long history of interpretation that views this passage as referring to worshipping God in the inner sphere of one's spirit rather than the temple, this is almost certainly not what John has in mind. Rather, in this passage John highlights the fact that the Holy Spirit will reveal Jesus' true identity as the Son of God to 'true worshippers'. Several factors suggest that this

---

[24] 心灵。
[25] Fee, 'Translational Tendenz', p. 355.
[26] 心灵。

reading is to be preferred over the readings advanced by the NIV and the *Union Version*.

First, the context is revealing. John 3.5 ('born of water and Spirit') sets the stage for the other key Spirit-passages in the early portion of the Gospel of John. Ezekiel 36.25-27, which associates water, cleansing, and a new heart for God with the Spirit, suggests that we should also interpret the collocation of water and Spirit in Jn 3.5 as a reference to the cleansing, transforming activity of the Spirit of God. This judgment finds confirmation in Jn 7.37-39 (see also Jn 4.10-14), a passage which establishes that, in John's perspective, 'living water' is a metaphor for the life-giving work of the Spirit. John 6.63, 'The Spirit gives life', also describes the Holy Spirit as the source of spiritual life. The context, then, indicates that we should understand πνεῦμα in Jn 4.23-24 as referring to the life-giving Spirit of God.

The fact that the two nouns, 'Spirit' and 'truth', are governed by one preposition (ἐν) is also significant, for it shows that the two are closely connected. When we add the observation that John elsewhere speaks of the 'Spirit of truth' (Jn 14.17; 15.26; 16.13), then our argument sharpens into focus. The context, the grammar, the references to 'Spirit of truth', all suggest that the phrase 'Spirit and truth' in Jn 4.23-24 should be understood as an example of hendiadys, the coordination of two ideas, one of which is dependent upon the other. Thus, in this passage John declares that the 'Spirit of truth' will reveal Jesus' true identity and the significance of the cross to the 'true worshippers' of God. Once again, we see that the *Union Version* fails to affirm the depth and richness of the human capacity to be led and taught by the Holy Spirit.

Revelation 19.10

Finally, we shall examine Rev. 19.10: 'For the testimony of Jesus is the spirit of prophecy' [ἡ γὰρ μαρτυρία 'Ιησοῦ ἐστιν τὸ πνεῦμα τῆς προφητείας]. Both the NIV and the *Union Version* understand πνεῦμα here to signify the 'essence' or 'heart' of the matter, which, in this case, is prophecy. Thus, the NIV translates, τὸ πνεῦμα τῆς προφητείας, as 'the spirit of prophecy'. The *Union Version* renders the phrase in a similar manner, utilizing a phrase that speaks of 'the essential or spiritual meaning of prophecy' (*yu yan zhong de ling yi*).[27] Both translations, then, understand the passage as a whole to affirm that, 'testimony about Jesus is the essence of prophecy'. Yet this reading of the passage is open to question. Let's take a closer look.

Several exegetical issues confront one seeking to interpret this important passage. First, how shall we understand the phrase, 'the testimony of Jesus' (ἡ μαρτυρία Ἰησοῦ)? If we read it as a subjective genitive, then the phrase refers to the 'testimony borne by Jesus'. If we see the phrase as an objective genitive, then it speaks of 'the testimony about Jesus' borne by others. Commentators divide over which interpretation is most fitting, but many recognize that we need not restrict the meaning of the phrase to only one of the options listed above. Indeed, as Stephen Smalley notes, the phrase very likely includes both elements, 'the testimony was given by Jesus to believers, who then handed it on to others'.[28] Nevertheless, in view of the usage of this phrase elsewhere in the Apocalypse (1.2, 9; 12.17; 19.10a), the phrase should be seen as 'primarily an objective genitive, referring to the church's testimony to Jesus'.[29] The immediate context also supports this reading. The striking statement, 'The testimony of Jesus is the spirit of prophecy', is uttered by an angel as he urges John the Revelator not to worship him, not to submit to idolatry (Rev. 19.9-10a). Of course the pressures to submit to false worship that confronted John's churches were great and included overt persecution. In this context, the phrase in question refers to 'testimony about Jesus uttered in the face of opposition and persecution'.

The English phrase utilized by the NIV, 'the testimony of Jesus', is ambiguous and may be interpreted as either an objective or a subjective genitive. However, the Chinese translation of the *Union Version* is unambiguous. It clearly and, in my view, correctly interprets the phrase, 'the testimony of Jesus' (ἡ μαρτυρία Ἰησοῦ), as an objective genitive. The Chinese text thus reads, 'The essence of prophecy is the testimony (borne by others) on behalf of Jesus.'

---

[27] Rev. 19.10: 因为预言中的灵意乃是为耶稣做见证。

[28] Stephen S. Smalley, *The Revelation to John: A Commentary on the Greek Text of the Apocalypse* (Downers Grove: InterVarsity Press, 2005), p. 487.

[29] Grant Osborne, *Revelation* (BECNT; Grand Rapids: Baker, 2002), p. 677.

A second question centers on the meaning of the phrase, 'the spirit of prophecy' (τὸ πνεῦμα τῆς προφητείας). As we have noted, the translators of the NIV and the Chinese *Union Version* understand πνεῦμα here to refer to 'essence' rather than the Spirit of God. Thus, the NIV does not capitalize 'spirit' and renders that passage with this force: 'the testimony of Jesus is the spirit [or essence] of prophecy'. The translators of the Chinese *Union Version* translate the passage at this point in a similar manner. Yet this reading of the text is almost certainly wrong. The literature of intertestamental Judaism routinely portrays the Holy Spirit as the source of prophetic inspiration. The association between the Spirit and prophecy was so strong that the Targums frequently translate references to the Spirit of God with the phrase 'the Spirit of prophecy'.[30] Additionally, Luke's emphasis on the Spirit as the source of prophetic inspiration (e.g. Acts 2.17-18) is echoed in John's Paraclete promises and elsewhere in the Apocalypse (e.g. numerous references to 'in the Spirit'). There can be little doubt, then, that with this phrase John the Revelator refers to 'Spirit-inspired prophecy.' Thus, the full sentence should be rendered: 'The testimony borne by others on behalf of Jesus (in the face of opposition and persecution), this is prophecy inspired by the Spirit of God.'

Conclusion

I have argued that the translators of the Chinese *Union Version* of the New Testament were uncomfortable with texts that refer to the Spirit of God speaking to, leading, or guiding followers of Jesus in very personal and subjective ways. They also appear to be reluctant to refer to the Spirit of God speaking through Christians. The *Union Version* translators were, of course, influenced by their own church tradition. Following the lead of Calvin and others in the Reformed tradition, they preferred to speak of God's communication with human beings as a rational process involving the study of Scripture. In short, they were, to a large extent, rationalists; and this rationalistic bias has influenced their translation of the New Testament at various points. More specifically, the *Un-*

---

[30] See the texts cited in Menzes, *Development*, pp. 99-104.

ion Version translators on numerous occasions have translated the term, πνεῦμα, as referring to the human spirit or related attitudes, when in fact the term should be understood as a reference to the Spirit of God.

Certainly we can understand the concerns of Calvin and his followers. Scripture must be our final authority. All of our subjective leadings must stand under its authority. But we must also resist the temptation to arc over into a form of sterile rationalism that discounts God's desire and his promise to speak to us, to lead us, and to guide us in very personal ways. Indeed, if the early Christians had simply relied on a rational analysis of the needs and opportunities before them, they would have never turned the world upside down for Jesus. They would have remained bound by their own prejudices and shackled by their fears. Can it be any different for us?

3

HOW SHALL WE TRANSLATE παράκλητος ?

In the latter part of John's gospel, we find three texts that speak of the Holy Spirit as the παράκλητος or Paraclete (Jn 14.16-26; 15.26-27; 16.7-15). The title παράκλητος is introduced here in the gospel for the first time and applied consistently to the Spirit of God in each of these texts (14.16, 26; 15.26; 16.7). Scholars have struggled to find a term that conveys the correct nuance of this important term. In their attempts to achieve some sort of dynamic equivalence, scholars have proposed a variety of translations. Titles such as 'comforter', 'exhorter', 'counselor', and 'helper' have all been used. The translators of the Chinese *Union Version* combine various ancient Chinese characters to create a new term, *bao hui shi*.[1] These characters, used by Confucian and Buddhist scholars long ago, designate a teacher or master who will nurture and bless a student or disciple. In this chapter I would like to suggest that all of these proposals miss the mark. It is my contention that if we are to understand the term παράκλητος and translate it accurately, we must first consider John's place in the process of development that marked the early church's under-

---

[1] 保惠师。 The oldest and most basic meaning of the term *bao*, 保, is to nurture or raise as one does with a child (see Xu Shen in the ancient Han dictionary, *Shuo Wen* [说文]). In *Zhao Gao* (召诰) of the Five Classics, the term is used with the sense of 'to bless and protect'. The term *hui* (惠) also carries the sense of 'to love in a nourishing way' (see again, Xu Shen's *Shuo Wen*). The term *shi* (师) is commonly used to speak of a religious master or teacher. Most modern Chinese would either not understand the term or think of a religious master or teacher who nurtures by giving guidance and protection.

standing of the work of the Holy Spirit. Then, we must examine
this specific title in the context of John's unique pneumatological
perspective. Only then shall we be able to arrive at a clear and accurate understanding of the Paraclete. To this task we now turn.

The Development of Early Christian Pneumatology

It is often assumed that from the very earliest days, the early
church had a unified and highly developed pneumatology.[2] Paul,
after all, writing from an early stage, offers a rich and full account
of the Spirit's work. And Paul, many would suggest, is simply
handing on what was already commonly known and accepted in
all of the churches. The Spirit was from the earliest days understood to be a soteriological agent, the source of cleansing (1 Cor.
6.11; Rom. 15.16), righteousness (Gal. 5.5 Rom. 8.1-17; Gal. 5.16-
26), intimate fellowship with (Gal. 4.6; Rom. 8.14-17) and knowl-
edge of God (1 Cor. 2.6-16; 2 Cor. 3.3-18), and ultimately, eternal
life through the resurrection (Rom. 8.11; 1 Cor. 15.42-49; Gal.
6.8).

There are good reasons, however, to question this reading of
the NT data. I have argued elsewhere that a thorough study of
Luke–Acts and the Pauline literature reveals that there was a process of development in the early church's understanding of the
Spirit's work. This, of course, is not a novel thesis and many
scholars from Hermann Gunkel to Gonzalo Haya-Prats have
reached similar conclusions.[3] My own study of the evidence, particularly in Luke–Acts,[4] led me to the following conclusions: Paul
was the first Christian to attribute soteriological functions to the
Spirit and his distinctive insights did not impact the non-Pauline

---

[2] See my review of the literature in Menzies, *The Development of Early Christian Pneumatology with special reference to Luke–Acts*, pp. 28-47.

[3] Hermann Gunkel, *The Influence of the Holy Spirit: the Popular View of the Ap-
ostolic Age and the Teaching of the Apostle Paul* (trans. R.A. Harrisville and P.A.
Quanbeck II; Philadelphia: Fortress Press, 1979; German Original, 1888); Gon-
zalo Haya-Prats, *L'Esprit force de l'église. Sa nature et son activité d'après les Actes des
Apôtres* (trans. J. Romero; LD, 81; Paris, Cerf, 1975); see also the sources cited in
Menzies, *Development*, pp. 18-28.

[4] See Menzies, *Development* and the slightly revised version, *Empowered for
Witness: The Spirit in Luke–Acts*(JPTSup 6; Sheffield: Sheffield Academic Press,
1994). See also William W. Menzies and Robert P. Menzies, *Spirit and Power:
Foundations of Pentecostal Experience* (Grand Rapids: Zondervan, 2000).

sectors of the early church until after the writing of Luke–Acts (ca. 70 CE). This conclusion is supported by the narrow focus of the pneumatology of the synoptic gospels and Acts.

Luke–Acts, with its wealth of material on the Spirit spanning both the ministry of Jesus and the beginnings of the early church, is especially important in this regard. I have argued that Luke consistently portrays the gift of the Spirit as a prophetic endowment that enables its recipient to fulfill a divinely ordained task. Whether it be John in his mother's womb, Jesus at the Jordan, or the disciples at Pentecost, the Spirit comes upon them all as the source of prophetic inspiration, granting special insight and inspiring speech. Thus Luke (like Matthew and Mark) does not present reception of the Spirit as necessary for one to enter into and remain with the community of salvation. In Luke's perspective, the disciples receive the Spirit, not as the source of cleansing and a new ability to keep the law, nor as the essential bond by which they are linked to God; rather, the disciples receive the Spirit as a prophetic *donum superadditum* that enables them to participate effectively in the missionary enterprise of the church.

I have also observed that the traditions of the primitive church utilized by Paul fail to attribute soteriological functions to the Spirit.[5] This observation, coupled with my analysis of Luke–Acts as described above, led me to conclude that the pneumatology of the early church was not as homogeneous as many have assumed. On the contrary, the evidence suggests that at least two distinct pneumatological perspectives co-existed: the 'prophetic' pneumatology of the primitive church (reflected in the synoptic gospels and Acts) and the 'soteriological' pneumatology of Paul. As noted above, it was not until after the writing of Luke–Acts (around 70 CE) that Paul's larger, fuller perspective began to impact wider, non-Pauline sectors of the church.

This reconstruction of the manner in which early Christian pneumatology took shape raises an interesting question: Where shall we place John's Gospel in this process of development? To this question we now turn.

---

[5] Menzies, *Development*, pp. 282-315.

The Johannine Synthesis

We begin our inquiry into the nature of John's contribution to the development of early Christian pneumatology by noting several facts. First, it is widely accepted that the Gospel of John was written in the last decade of the first century CE (the 90s), significantly later than Paul's epistles (roughly 48-64 CE) and Luke–Acts (70 CE). Secondly, we may observe that John not only writes from this later date, he also provides more theological interpretation than the synoptic gospels as he relates the story of Jesus.[6] Thirdly, John has clearly absorbed the pneumatological insights of both Paul[7] and the non-Pauline primitive church and he presents his gospel from this broader theological perspective.[8] This explains, at least partially, why the Spirit features more prominently in John than the other gospels. It also explains, I would add, why John (unlike the synoptic gospels) presents the Spirit, not simply as the impulse of prophetic inspiration, but also as a soteriological agent.

If these observations and our reconstruction outlined above are correct, it would appear that the Gospel of John represents a synthesis of the pneumatology of the primitive, non-Pauline church and that of Paul. Indeed, we shall argue that this is precisely the case. Furthermore, we shall argue that John's pneumatological synthesis validates our reconstruction of the development of early Christian pneumatology as outlined above and that it offers insight into how the prophetic and soteriological pneumatologies were integrated in the early church. This insight will, in turn, help us answer our central question: How shall we translate παράκλητος? Let us begin by looking at the various pneumatological strands in John's Gospel.

---

[6] George Ladd speaks for many when he concludes that 'John reflects a larger measure of theological interpretation than do the Synoptics' (G. Ladd, *A Theology of the New Testament* [ed. Donald A. Hagner; Grand Rapids: Eerdmans, 1993 revised edition], p. 257).

[7] U. Schnelle argues that the Pauline tradition reached John's school through oral tradition and that this transmission of tradition reflects a dominant geographical environment, probably Ephesus. See U. Schnelle, 'Paulus und Johannes', *Evangelische Theologie* 47 (1987), pp. 212-28.

[8] John's parenthetical comment in Jn 7.39 illustrates this fact and may offer insight into John's method.

The Life-Giving Spirit

John describes the Spirit as the source of spiritual life in four key texts in the early part of his gospel: 3.5-8; 4.23-24; 6.63; and 7.37-39. Our purpose here is not to offer a detailed study of each of these passages; rather, we shall simply note that these passages, in a manner similar to Paul, attribute soteriological functions to the Spirit. John 3.5-8 illustrates the point well.

Jesus' reference to a birth of 'water and the Spirit' (3.5) has generated numerous interpretations. But Max Turner correctly notes that the grammatical structure (a single preposition governs the two nouns connected by καὶ) indicates that the phrase does not speak of two, distinct births; rather, the phrase 'born of water and the Spirit' describes a single birth accomplished through a combination of water and Spirit.[9] This fact narrows the possible interpretations considerably by ruling out interpretations that feature two distinct births (e.g. water signifying physical birth; spirit, spiritual birth). In view of Jesus' rebuke of Nicodemus in v. 10, 'You are Israel's teacher ... and you do not understand these things?', it is evident that we should look to the Old Testament for insight into the text. Most scholars see Ezek. 36.25-27, with its collocation of water and Spirit, as forming the backdrop for Jesus words:[10]

> I will sprinkle clean water on you, and you will be clean; I will cleanse you from all your impurities and from all your idols. I will give you a new heart and put a new spirit in you; I will remove from you your heart of stone and give you a heart of flesh. And I will put my Spirit in you and move you to follow my decrees and be careful to keep my laws. (Ezek. 36: 25-27).

Ezekiel 36.25-27, which associates water, cleansing, and a new heart for God with the Spirit, indicates that we should also inter-

---

[9] Max Turner, *The Holy Spirit and Spiritual Gifts in the New Testament Church and Today* (Peabody, Mass: Hendrickson, 1998 revised edition), p. 68.

[10] See for example Raymond Brown, *The Gospel According to John* Vol. 1 (The Anchor Bible 29; Garden City, N.Y.: Doubleday & Co, Inc., 1966), p. 140; J. Ramsey Michaels, *John* (NIBC 4; Peabody, Mass: Hendrickson, 1989), p. 61; Bruce Milne, *The Message of John* (BST; Leicester: Inter-Varsity Press, 1993), p. 76; and Linda Belleville, '"Born of Water and Spirit": John 3.5', *Trinity Journal* 1 (1980), pp. 125-41.

pret the collocation of water and Spirit in Jn 3.5 as a reference to the cleansing, transforming activity of the Spirit of God. This judgment is supported by Jn 7.37-39, which establishes that, in John's perspective, 'living water' is a metaphor for the life-giving work of the Spirit.

The reference to a birth of 'water and the Spirit' (3.5) then clarifies further Jesus declaration to Nicodemus, 'I tell you the truth, unless a man is born from above, he cannot see the Kingdom of God' (Jn 3.3).[11] Jesus affirms that spiritual life, which only comes from God (above), is necessary for entrance into the Kingdom of God, and that this life is generated in the believer through the Holy Spirit (3.5). We conclude that John, drawing upon Ezek. 36.25-27, presents the Spirit as a soteriological agent in Jn 3.5.[12]

John 3.5 sets the stage for the other key Spirit-passages in the early portion of the Gospel of John. John 6.63, 'The Spirit gives life', and Jn 7.37-39, which identifies 'living water' with the Spirit, also describe the Spirit as the source of spiritual life. John 4.23-24 is a bit more cryptic, yet here again it would seem that the Spirit is presented as a soteriological agent. In view of the larger context of John's Gospel and the collocation of Spirit and truth in this specific text, Jn 4.23-24 probably refers to the Spirit as the agent who reveals Jesus' true identity and the significance of the cross to the 'true worshipers.' In each of these four passages (3.5-8; 4.23-24; 6.63; and 7.37-39), then, John emphasizes the Spirit's role as the source of spiritual life.

The Paraclete

In the latter part of John's Gospel, in the midst of Jesus' farewell discourse, we find three texts which speak of the Holy Spirit as the Paraclete (Jn 14.16-26; 15.26-27; 16.7-15). The term παρά-κλητος, introduced here in the gospel for the first time and applied consistently to the Spirit in each of these texts (14.16, 26;

---

[11] There the term ἄνωθεν (Jn 3.3) can mean 'again' or 'from above'. Here both meanings are probably in view. For this reason, I have followed the variant reading of the NIV, 'born from above', in this translation.

[12] It is interesting to note that Ezek. 36.26 and perhaps Ezek. 37.14 form the backdrop for Paul's references to the Spirit as source of new covenant existence in 2 Cor. 3.1-6. Luke, on the other hand, does not draw upon Ezekiel 36-37 to elucidate the work of the Spirit.

15.26; 16.7), suggests that John has something special in mind. Clearly here the Spirit is described in a unique way. Could it be that with this new title John designates a new and distinctive dimension of the Spirit's work? Let us examine the evidence.

A review of the Greek literature reveals that the term παράκλητος refers to 'one called alongside', an advocate, who offers counsel and assistance in a court or dispute.[13] This meaning accords well with the manner in which the term is used in 1 Jn 2.1, the only other place the term occurs in the NT outside of John's gospel. In spite of this evidence, many have felt that the functions attributed to the Paraclete in John 14-16 are not consistent with this forensic setting and the associated sense of 'advocate'. Other explanations of the term have been put forward, including 'comforter', 'exhorter', 'counselor', and 'helper.' As we noted above, the Chinese *Union Version* chooses to utilize an ancient and relatively unknown term designating a teacher or master. Yet, as Anthony Billington observes, 'the vast majority of the studies drive us back to a primary forensic context' for the term.[14]

Billington, citing several recent studies, notes that throughout his gospel John features a trial motif. This motif is accentuated by the use of courtroom terminology, especially the term 'witness'.[15] It is also advanced by the discourses within the gospel, where various parties question and interrogate one another and their explanations. The trial motif carries over into Jesus' farewell discourse, which forms the context for the Paraclete sayings. In John 14-16, then, Jesus reassures the disciples that, in spite of his im-

---

[13] J. Behm, in his study of the term Paraclete, concludes: 'Thus the history of the term in the whole sphere of known Greek and Hellenistic usage outside the NT yields the clear picture of a legal advisor or helper or advocate in the relevant court' (J. Behm, 'παράκλητος', in *TDNT*, V, p. 803).

[14] Anthony Billington, 'The Paraclete and Mission in the Fourth Gospel', p. 94 in A. Billington, T. Lane, and M. Turner (eds.), *Mission and Meaning: Essays Presented to Peter Cotterell* (Carlisle: Paternoster Press, 1995), pp. 90-115. Note also the conclusion of G. Burge: 'This context of juridical trial and persecution presents us with the most likely catalyst for John's introduction of the term ὁ παράκλητος' (Burge, *The Anointed Community: The Holy Spirit in the Johannine Community* [Grand Rapids: Eerdmans, 1987], p. 205).

[15] Of the over 200 occurrences in the NT of μάρτυς ('witness') and its cognates, approximately 40% are found in the Johannine literature (John, 1-3 John, and Revelation). More specifically, μαρτυρέω ('testify') occurs 76 times in the NT and 33 times in the Gospel of John. The term μαρτυρία ('testimony') occurs 37 times in the NT and 14 times in the Gospel of John.

minent departure, they will not be left alone. Jesus will send the Paraclete, another advocate, who will aid them in the cosmic trial already underway between Jesus and the unbelieving world.[16] Let us examine how the Paraclete functions as an advocate in this cosmic trial.

The forensic functions of the Paraclete are clearly evident in Jn 15.26-27 and 16.5-16. In Jn 15.26-27 we read:

> When the Paraclete comes, whom I will send to you from the Father, the Spirit of truth who goes out from the Father, he will testify about me; but you also must testify, for you have been with me from the beginning.

This passage appears in a setting that highlights the world's rejection of Jesus and his disciples: 'If they persecuted me, they will persecute you also' (Jn 15.20). The world's rejection of Christ, even in the face of his words (15.22) and deeds (15.24), establishes its guilt. The repeated references to conflict, guilt, and witness establish the forensic character of the passage.

The specific function ascribed to the Paraclete is that of a witness. He will testify concerning Christ (15.26).[17] This can only mean that he will seek to persuade the world that it unjustly rejected and crucified Jesus, who is in reality the Son of God, God's agent of salvation. This theme is developed more fully in Jn 16.8-11:

> When he comes, he will convict the world of guilt in regard to sin and righteousness and judgment: in regard to sin, because men do not believe in me; in regard to righteousness, because I am going to the Father, where you can see me no longer; and in regard to judgment, because the prince of this world now stands condemned.

Although this passage contains numerous exegetical difficulties, the essential meaning is relatively clear. The Paraclete will press home his case against the world: first, that its rejection (unbelief) of Christ is the essence of its sin; secondly, that although the

---

[16] Billington, 'Paraclete and Mission', p. 100; for the trial motif see pp. 95-101.
[17] Revelation 19.10, 'For the testimony of Jesus is the spirit of prophecy', forms a striking parallel to Jn 15.26.

world crucified Jesus as a criminal, his death, resurrection, and exaltation vindicate him as the Righteous One; thirdly, Jesus' vindication establishes that those who oppose him already stand condemned.[18] The Paraclete, then, will bear witness against the world. It is important to note, however, that the Spirit as the Paraclete will do this, 'not by some inward testimony in the hearts of the people of the world, but by the outward testimony of words spoken by Jesus' disciples in the course of their mission.'[19] The Paraclete is given to the disciples to be *their* advocate; that is, to support *their* witness to the world.[20] This is also the point of Jn 15.26-27: 'he [the Paraclete] will testify about me; but you [the disciples] also must testify.'[21] Note the following verses, Jn 16.1-4, which emphasize that the Paraclete's role is to enable the disciples to stand firm in the face of persecution and, in this setting, to testify boldly about Jesus.[22]

The fact that the Paraclete comes to encourage and enable the witness of the disciples is further highlighted in Jn 14.16-26 and 16.12-15. In Jn 14.16 we read that Jesus will send 'another Paraclete' to assist the disciples. This indicates that Jesus during his earthly ministry has served as a Paraclete. In view of the trial motif running throughout John's Gospel, Billington correctly stresses that the work of the Spirit and Jesus at this point are one and the same: to confront a hostile world.[23] This is precisely why the disciples will not be orphans (14.18). Left on their own, they would be helpless, unable to prosecute their case against the world. But with the Spirit as their advocate, they will not be alone. Indeed, the Spirit as Paraclete will teach them 'all things' and remind them of everything Jesus had said (14.26). So also Jn 16.12-15 declares that the Paraclete will guide the disciples 'into all truth'.[24] In this forensic context, these words take on a specific meaning. The Spirit will

---

[18] Cf. John 12.30-32. See Turner, *The Holy Spirit and Spiritual Gifts*, p. 87.

[19] Michaels, *John*, p. 282.

[20] See also Turner, *The Holy Spirit and Spiritual Gifts*, p. 87.

[21] Billington, 'Paraclete and Mission', p. 109: 'The Paraclete's work is not independent of their witness. John does not teach a witness by the Spirit that is not also a witness through the believing community.'

[22] Michaels, *John*, p. 277.

[23] Billington, 'Paraclete and Mission', 109-110.

[24] John 16.13-15 also suggests that the Paraclete will guide the church in its mission ('tell you what is yet to come'). The stress on the authority of Jesus is very similar to what we find in Mt. 28.18.

help the disciples recall and understand important aspects of Jesus' teaching so that they may press home their case against the world (i.e. witness effectively).[25]

It is important at this juncture to note the similarities and differences between the functions of the Spirit as Paraclete in John 14-16 and the life-giving Spirit in John 3-7. Although both the Paraclete and life-giving Spirit convey wisdom, the nature and purpose of this wisdom is quite distinct. The life-giving Spirit enables its recipients to grasp the significance of the cross and Jesus' true identity. The Paraclete, on the other hand, given to disciples *in order to assist their witness,* offers charismatic wisdom by enabling the disciples to recall and understand the teaching of Jesus. The purpose of the Paraclete is not to grant the disciples that wisdom which is essential for right relationship with God (i.e. spiritual life). Rather, the Paraclete grants a special kind of wisdom; it is wisdom that is directed toward the unbelieving world in the form of witness.

In short, we have argued that the trial context of John's Gospel in general and, more specifically, the forensic terminology in the Paraclete passages, call us to recognize the Paraclete's distinctive role and function. He comes to the disciples as their advocate, one who assists them in presenting the case of Christ against the world. He accomplishes this task by encouraging and enabling bold witness in the face of opposition and persecution. Although the Paraclete grants wisdom – he helps the disciples recall and understand the teaching of Jesus – this wisdom is ultimately directed toward the world. Thus, it is charismatic rather than soteriological (i.e. essential for right relationship with God) in nature and should be distinguished from the life-giving wisdom imparted by the Spirit in John 3–7.

This conclusion, particularly that John distinguishes between the functions of the Spirit as the Paraclete and those of the life-giving Spirit in John 3–7, is supported by Jn 20.22.

---

[25] In view of the forensic setting, 'all things' (14.26) and 'all truth' (16.13) probably refer to all that the disciples will need to know in order to prosecute their case against the world. The conceptual parallels with Lk. 12.11-12 are striking.

John 20.22

John 20.22 describes a pre-ascension bestowal of the Spirit with these words: 'And with that he breathed on them and said, "Receive the Holy Spirit".' This text raises problems for those who have attempted to understand Pentecost as the climax of conversion, the moment when the disciples were regenerated by the power of the Spirit. How does one relate Jn 20.22, with its pre-ascension bestowal of the Spirit, to Pentecost? Some have sought to deny that an impartation of the Spirit was actually given.[26] The text is said to describe a purely symbolic act that anticipates Pentecost. This view has been largely rejected by contemporary scholars as a forced attempt to reconcile John's narrative with Acts.[27] Others have suggested that this event is, for John, his equivalent to Pentecost.[28] On this view John is not overly concerned with chronology and it is best to let John be John. The weakness of this view lies in the fact that it is virtually certain that John and his audience would have known of Pentecost. Why would John present a picture of Pentecost that would raise many questions and lead to confusion? I believe there is a better way to understand this passage, one that places it within the framework of John's larger narrative.

To begin with, we must recognize that this passage describes the disciples' reception of the life-giving Spirit. The verb John uses, ἐνεφύσησεν, which is translated 'he breathed', is exceptionally rare. This verb, however, is found in Gen. 2.7 where it describes God's breathing into Adam the breath of life.[29] This careful use of language would undoubtedly remind John's readers of the creation account. The point of the parallel could not be

---

[26] See for example D.A. Carson, *The Gospel According to John* (Leicester: Inter-Varsity Press, 1991), pp. 649-52 and J.I. Packer, *Keep in Step with the Spirit* (Old Tappan, NJ: Fleming H. Revell, 1984), pp. 87-88.

[27] Thus, most scholars see this as an actual bestowal of the Spirit. See for example J. Dunn, *Baptism*, p. 178 and M. Turner, *The Holy Spirit and Spiritual Gifts*, pp. 91-92.

[28] See for example R. Brown, *The Gospel According to John* Vol. 2, pp. 1022-1024, 1036-45 and George T. Montague, *The Holy Spirit: Growth of a Biblical Tradition* (New York: Paulist Press, 1976), p. 363.

[29] The verb is also found in Wisd. 15.11, which is essentially a citation of Gen. 2.7, and in Ezek. 37.9, which refers to God's breathing into the dry bones of Israel the breath of life. The Ezek. 37.9 reference is important in that here, too, we see the verb associated with the creation of new life.

missed. Just as God breathed into Adam the breath of life, so also Jesus now breathes into the disciples the Spirit of new creation. The imperative, 'Receive the Holy Spirit', in this context would naturally be understood to signify that the life-giving Spirit was actually imparted.

One might argue that the context of Jn 20.21-23, particularly the sending formula ('As the Father hath sent me, I am sending you'), points beyond the regenerating work of the Spirit to an empowering for witness. However, in view of the allusion to Gen. 2.7, it is certainly better to see here a bestowal of the Spirit of new creation, which was the necessary condition for reception of Pentecostal power. Since John does not describe the bestowal of the Pentecostal gift, here with the contextual markers, he points toward its future coming.[30] This judgment is supported by the lack of any Paraclete activity, at least with reference to the disciples, in the passages that immediately follow. As Turner notes, far from offering bold and dynamic witness, the disciples 'fail to convince Thomas, let alone "the world".'[31]

We have already noted that Jn 7.37-39 anticipates a bestowal of the life-giving Spirit to the disciples. There are a number of reasons to view this event (20.22) as the fulfillment of the promise of the life-giving Spirit in Jn 7.39 and not the fulfillment of the promise of the Paraclete. First, there is the linguistic evidence. John 7.39 speaks of the disciples 'receiving' the Spirit. In Jn 20.22, Jesus uses the same verb to form his imperative: 'Receive the Holy Spirit'. The verbal parallels here may be contrasted with the general tendency to identify the Paraclete as a gift that issues from the Father. Whereas in Jn 20.22 Jesus breathes upon the disciples and bestows the Spirit; the Paraclete is a gift the Father gives (14.16) and the one whom the Father will send in Jesus' name (14.26). Alternatively, Jesus says that he will send the Paraclete (16.7) and he will send the Paraclete 'from the Father' (15.26). Jesus also notes that the Paraclete (now, the Spirit of truth) 'goes out from the Father' (15.26). Although admittedly the picture is not entirely clear,

---

[30] B.F. Westcott, *The Gospel According to St. John* (Grand Rapids: Eerdmans, 1954), p. 295: Westcott describes the bestowal of the Spirit in Jn 20.22 as 'the necessary condition for the descent of the Holy Spirit on the day of Pentecost.'
[31] Turner, *The Holy Spirit and Spiritual Gifts*, p. 95.

the descriptions of the Father's sending or giving of the Paraclete do not fit well with a fulfillment in Jn 20.22.

Second and more decisive is the matter of timing. John 7.39 indicates that the life-giving Spirit 'had not been given, since Jesus had not yet been glorified'. Since for John Jesus' glorification generally refers to the death and the resurrection of Jesus,[32] this promise accords well with the post-resurrection (pre-ascension) fulfillment in Jn 20.22. The Paraclete promises, however, indicate that the Paraclete will come, indeed can come, only after Jesus has ascended to the Father. This is stated most clearly in Jn 16.7: 'But I tell you the truth: It is for your good that I am going away. Unless I go away, the Counselor [παράκλητος] will not come to you; but if I go, I will send him to you' (cf. 14.18-19; 16.7). These temporal markers indicate that in John's view, the life-giving Spirit is received by the disciples in Jn 20.22 and that this bestowal of the Spirit cannot be equated with the sending of the Paraclete. The Paraclete can come only after Jesus ascends to the Father.

Thirdly, our judgment is supported by the distinctive functions attributed to the life-giving Spirit of John 3-7 and the Paraclete of John 14-16. We have already noted that the Spirit in John 3-7 comes as the source of regeneration. By way of contrast, the Paraclete comes to the disciples in order to enable their testimony on behalf of Christ.

Together, these points indicate that Jn 20.22 records a pre-ascension bestowal of the life-giving Spirit. The evidence also suggests that, from John's perspective, Jn 20.22 represents the fulfillment of the promise of Jn 7.37-39. Yet this gift of the Spirit should be distinguished from the Paraclete passages, which ascribe different functions to the Spirit and which find their fulfillment at Pentecost.

---

[32] The term δοξάζω occurs 23 times in John's Gospel. When John speaks of the glorification of Jesus, he often has in mind Jesus' death on the cross (12.23; 12.27-28; 13.31-32; 17.1). In Jn 12.16 Jesus' glorification most likely refers to the death and resurrection of Jesus, and this is probably the case in Jn 7.39 as well. For a similar assessment of Jn 7.39 see G.R. Beasley-Murray, *John* Vol. 1 (Word Biblical Commentary 36; Waco: Word, 1987), p. 117.

John and the Development of Early Christian Pneumatology

It is perhaps worth noting that, up to this point, our conclusions are very similar to those of James Dunn. Dunn also argues that Jn 20.22 is a fulfillment of the Spirit promises in John 3-7 and that this bestowal of the Spirit should be distinguished from the promise of the Paraclete, which is fulfilled at Pentecost.[33] This position, of course, is not unique to Dunn.[34] Others, such as Max Turner, also argue that John had in mind two bestowals of the Spirit: one at Jn 20.22; and one at Pentecost. Nevertheless, both Dunn and Turner stress the theological unity of these bestowals of the Spirit, suggesting that both bestowals are of the same character.[35] Yet this understanding of John raises a number of questions.

We may begin by asking, if John actually viewed both bestowals of the Spirit (Jn 20.22 and Pentecost) as representing essentially one theological impartation of the Spirit, why does he separate them chronologically? Dunn and Turner cannot provide a clear rationale for John's narrative at this point. This is especially the case since both view the two receptions of the Spirit as functioning in essentially the same manner. Dunn suggests that John distinguishes between the two gifts because they represent distinctive milestones in salvation-history: 'what we now call full Christian experience was possible only after the ascension and Pentecost.'[36] Undoubtedly, in John's perspective, the Paraclete could not come until after Pentecost. Yet how was it distinct from the bestowal recorded in Jn 20.22? Dunn's reference to 'full Christian experience' suggests that Pentecost represents something more, something different. However, in view of the regeneration language in Jn 20.22, Dunn is unable to articulate what this 'more' actually is. The same may be said of Turner, who states emphatically that we cannot distinguish between the functions of the Spirit imparted to the disciples in Jn 20.22 and those of the Para-

---

[33] Dunn, *Baptism*, pp. 176-82.

[34] See for example B.F. Westcott, *John*, p. 295 and Howard Ervin, *Spirit Baptism: A Biblical Investigation* (Peabody: Mass.: Hendrickson, 1987), pp. 14-21.

[35] Dunn, *Baptism*, pp. 181-82 and Turner, *The Holy Spirit and Spiritual Gifts*, pp. 99-100.

[36] Dunn, *Baptism*, p. 181.

clete.[37] So, we are still left with the fundamental question unan-
swered: why would John speak of two experiences of regeneration
by the Spirit? Put another way, if the Pentecostal gift is indeed the
climax of conversion-initiation, why detail another bestowal of
the Spirit that functions in essentially the same way?

This question becomes all the more acute when we remember
that John did not have to record the Jn 20.22 bestowal of the
Spirit; none of the other gospel-writers do, why does he? Surely
John, writing in the 90's, would have recognized the confusion an
account of a pre-Pentecostal bestowal of the life-giving Spirit
would cause? What is now clear is that traditional accounts of the
development of early Christian pneumatology, particularly those
that stress the homogeneity of Luke and Paul, are simply unable
to explain in an intelligible manner John's narrative.

The answer to this riddle is, however, easily explained if we
place John within the process of the development of early Christian pneumatology outlined above. If Paul was indeed the first
Christian to articulate the soteriological aspects of the Spirit's
work and his broader perspective did not impact the more limited,
prophetic pneumatology of the non-Pauline church until after the
writing of the synoptic gospels and Acts, then we can see John as
providing a later synthesis of these two pneumatological strands.
Clearly John is aware of Paul's larger perspective, as is obvious by
John's references to the life-giving Spirit (John 3-7). This being the
case, it is only natural that John would seek to answer a question
not addressed in the synoptic gospels: When did the disciples receive the Spirit as a regenerating force (the Pauline gift of the
Spirit)? Since the synoptic gospels and Acts represent an early
stage in the early church's developing awareness of the Spirit's
work and know the Spirit only as the source of prophetic inspiration (e.g. the Pentecostal gift of Acts 2), they would not have pondered this question. But after Paul's insights had become more
widely known, then the question and the need to address it would
have arisen. In the 90's, John writes his gospel from this larger
pneumatological perspective, and so he seeks to answer this criti-

---

[37] Turner, *The Holy Spirit and Spiritual Gifts*, pp. 100-101. Turner suggests that
the Paraclete comes 'as the means of [Jesus'] continued presence with the disciples' and as 'one who … illumines the Christ-event' (p. 100). Yet Turner also
attributes these functions to the life-giving Spirit of John 3-7.

cal question. His answer is straightforward: John 20.22 marks the moment when the disciples received the life-giving Spirit; this experience is distinct from the later bestowal of the Paraclete (i.e. the Pentecostal gift), which enables the disciples to bear witness for Christ. John then offers a synthesis: a later perspective on the life of Jesus, informed by Paul's richer pneumatology – one that, in contrast to Luke, identifies the Spirit as the source of new life and tells us when the disciples actually experienced the regenerating power of the Spirit.[38]

Conclusion

I have argued that John, writing in the 90s and fully aware of the prophetic pneumatology of the synoptic gospels and Acts as well as Paul's broader perspective, provides a striking synthesis. His synthesis affirms that the Spirit comes as a regenerating force (Jn 20.22) and that, in a theologically distinct experience, the Spirit (as the Paraclete) is also received as the power which enables the disciples to bear witness for Christ. John's perspective, then, challenges reconstructions of early Christian pneumatology that do not allow for diversity and development.

John's pneumatology also calls into question the numerous attempts to translate παράκλητος with vague, non-forensic titles. Translations such as 'comforter', 'exhorter', 'counselor', 'helper', and the Chinese *Union Version's* 'teacher' (*bao hui shi*), all miss the mark. They ignore the fact that 'the history of the term in the whole sphere of known Greek and Hellenistic usage outside the NT yields the clear picture of a legal advisor or helper or advocate in the relevant court.'[39] They also lose sight of the context of John's gospel, which, with its extended 'trial motif', also suggests that παράκλητος should be understood in a legal or forensic sense. But, most importantly, they fail to comprehend John's pneumatological perspective. As John's paradigm for Pentecost,

---

[38] This understanding of John's pneumatology takes seriously the historicity of Luke's account of Pentecost (Acts 2) and represents an alternative assessment of the evidence to that proposed by G. Twelftree, who maintains that Luke created it. See Twelftree, *People of the Spirit: Exploring Luke's View of the Church* (Grand Rapids: Baker, 2009), pp. 65-83.

[39] J. Behm, 'παράκλητος', *TDNT*, V, p. 803.

the Paraclete comes to the disciples as their 'advocate', one who assists them in presenting the case of Christ against the unbelieving world.

4

IS THE KINGDOM OF GOD WITHIN YOU?

Pentecostals the world over celebrate the present-ness of the kingdom of God. God's awesome presence in our midst, his gracious willingness to bestow spiritual gifts, his desire to heal, liberate, and transform lives – all of these themes, so central to Pentecostal piety, highlight the fact that God's reign is now present. Pentecostals proclaim a God who is near, a God whose power can and should be experienced here and now. This element of Pentecostal praxis has, for the most part, served as a much-needed corrective to traditional church life, which has far too often lost sight of the manifest presence of God. In a deeply moving essay, Ulrich Luz acknowledges this fact when he declares, 'Now we worry about the fact that living religion has to a large extent emigrated from the mainstream churches and flourishes elsewhere … in living communities of neocharismatic groups, in colourful open-air meetings, and so on … the future belongs to religion and not to the traditional Christian churches.'[1]

As traditional churches in the West have increasingly lost touch with the supernatural elements of the Christian faith, Pentecostals have reveled in their worship of an immanent God, a God who speaks to us, a God who is truly with us. Although many in an increasingly secular West struggle to understand this kind of faith, Pentecostal churches around the world are growing with such ra-

---

[1] Ulrich Luz, 'Paul as Mystic' in Graham N. Stanton, Bruce W. Longenecker, and Stephen C. Barton (eds.), *The Holy Spirit and Christian Origins: Essays in Honor of James D.G. Dunn* (Grand Rapids: William B. Eerdmans, 2004), p. 131.

pidity that one scholar has suggested that the Pentecostal movement should be identified as 'the most successful social movement
of the past century.'[2] Like it or not, the Pentecostal movement is
shaping the contours of Christian faith and praxis throughout the
world.

In the following chapter I would like to examine a text that
speaks of this 'present-ness of the kingdom of God' that Pentecostals celebrate. However, the force of this text is often blunted
by what I believe to be a mistranslation of Luke's language. The
text in question, Lk. 17.20-21, reads:

Once, having been asked by the Pharisees when the kingdom
of God would come, Jesus replied, 'The kingdom of God does
not come with your careful observation, nor will people say,
'Here it is', or 'There it is', because the kingdom of God is
within you.'

The key words that we wish to consider are found in v. 21, 'the
kingdom of God is within you (ἡ βασιλεία τοῦ θεοῦ ἐντὸς
ὑμῶν ἐστιν)'. In particular, we shall question the way in which
the NIV translates ἐντὸς ὑμῶν with the phrase 'within you'. This
translation is found in various other English translations, including
the KJV, the TEV, and the translations of J.B. Phillips and William
Barclay.[3] The translators of the Chinese *Union Version* also follow

---

[2] Philip Jenkins, *The Next Christendom: The Coming of Global Christianity* (Oxford: Oxford University Press, 2002), p. 8. Of course, in the midst of this
growth and exuberance, Pentecostals face a very present danger. The emphases
that have enabled Pentecostals to make a unique contribution, also render us
susceptible to an unbalanced triumphalism. Our vision can (and often has) become so fixated on God's power and triumph that we lose the ability to see his
hand in the midst of suffering, rejection, and opposition. Our emphasis on the
present-ness of the kingdom is easily twisted into an arrogant and unbiblical
over-realized eschatology, where there is little room for weakness. Luther
named it well: a 'theology of glory' that had little room for a 'theology of the
cross'. See Veli-Matti Kärkkäinen, 'Theology of the Cross: A Stumbling Block
to Pentecostal/Charismatic Spirituality?' in Wonsuk Ma and Robert Menzies,
eds., *The Spirit and Spirituality: Essays in Honour of Russell P. Spittler* (JPTSup 24;
London: T&T Clark International, 2004), pp. 150-63. Martin Mittelstadt offers
an antidote for this danger in his fine study, *The Spirit and Suffering in Luke–Acts:
Implications for a Pentecostal Pneumatology* (JPTSup 26; London: T&T Clark International, 2004).

[3] See *The New Testament in Modern English*, translated by J.B. Phillips (New
York: The MacMillan Co., 1958). Phillips' translation reads: 'for the kingdom of

this approach and thus render ἐντος ὑμῶν with the phrase, *zai nimen xin li*,[4] which also means 'within you' or 'in your hearts'.

This translation suggests that, according to Jesus, the kingdom of God is something that is not visible, something that is purely internal or spiritual. The kingdom of God, according to this reading, 'works in men's hearts'.[5] But is this quiet, invisible, ethereal, and unobtrusive kingdom really the kingdom that Jesus proclaimed and inaugurated? Are Pentecostals wrong to highlight the powerful presence of God now at work in our midst through healings, exorcisms, prophecy, and other visible manifestations? Or perhaps, at the very least, Pentecostals should look elsewhere for support for their exuberant practices.

However, before we rush too quickly to this conclusion, we need to acknowledge that this reading of Lk. 17.21 has not gone unchallenged. Numerous others English translations follow a different line of interpretation. They translate ἐντος ὑμῶν with the words, 'among you'.[6] This translation represents a significant shift in meaning from that of the NIV and The Chinese *Union Version* and, as we shall argue, for contextual reasons is to be preferred.

We shall begin our study by examining the larger context of Luke–Acts, and then focus on the immediate context of Lk. 17.21. We shall also note the significant implications that flow from our suggested translation.

The Larger Context: The Kingdom of God in Luke–Acts

Continuity in Luke–Acts

It has been increasingly recognized that in the New Testament the kingdom of God is understood to be both a present and a future

---

God is inside you' (p. 163). Note also William Barclay, *The Gospel of Luke* (The Daily Study Bible Series; Philadelphia, Westminster Press, rev. edn, 1975), p. 219: 'the kingdom of God is within you.'

  [4] 在你们心里。

  [5] Barclay, *Luke*, p. 220.

  [6] See for example the *New Revised Standard Version*, the *Revised English Bible*, the *New American Bible*, and the *New Jerusalem Bible*. So also Eugene Peterson, in *The Message*, whose translation reads, 'God's kingdom is already among you'.

reality.[7] George Ladd correctly notes that the most distinctive aspect of Jesus' preaching recorded in the synoptic gospels 'was its
present in-breaking in history in his own person and mission'.[8]
This is undoubtedly the case in Luke's Gospel. The kingdom is
both a present realm of redemptive blessing (Lk. 4.21; 10.18;
11.20; 16.16; 22.29) and a future eschatological reality (Lk. 13.28-
29; 19.11).[9]

In Luke's Gospel the terms most commonly used to describe
this realm of redemptive blessing are 'salvation' (σωτήιον,
σωτηρία, σῴζω) and 'forgiveness' (ἄφεσις).[10] That Jesus is the
source of this salvation is clear from the very outset of the gospel
(Lk. 1.69, 71, 77; 2.30). Entrance into this realm of redemptive
blessing is contingent on a response of 'faith' (πίστις) to Jesus'
message. This is clear from the way Luke connects the verb 'to
save' (σῴζω) with 'faith' (πίστις), indicating that salvation is contingent on a response of faith (Lk. 7.50; 8.12, 50; 17.19; 18.42).
That this redemption is experienced, at least in part, in the present
is evident by Luke's use of σῴζω in the perfect tense (Lk. 7.50;
17.18; 18.42). Although salvation has a future referent, it is experienced in the present.

Acts shows direct continuity with these characteristics of the
kingdom of God emphasized in Luke's Gospel. It is true that in
Acts kingdom terminology is increasingly replaced by other ways
of expressing the salvation provided by Jesus. But this is the result

---

[7] See the works by W.G. Kümmel, *Promise and Fulfillment* (London: SCM
Press, 1957); O. Cullmann, *Christ and Time* (Philadelphia: Westminster, 1964);
H.N. Ridderbos, *The Coming of the Kingdom* (Phildaelphia: Reformed and Presbyterian, 1962); R. Schnackenburg, *God's Rule and Kingdom* (Montreal: Palm, 1963);
G.E. Ladd, *A Theology of the New Testament* (revised edition; Grand Rapids: William B. Eerdmans, 1993) and *The Presence of the Future* (Grand Rapids: Eerdmans, 1974).

[8] Ladd, *A Theology of the New Testament*, p. 70.

[9] I agree with G.E. Ladd when he declares, 'God's rule' is 'the best point of
departure for understanding' the Kingdom of God in the gospels (Ladd, *A
Theology of the New Testament*, pp. 60-61; see also Ladd, 'The Kingdom of God –
Reign or Realm?', *Journal of Biblical Literature* 81 [1962], pp. 230-38). However,
'God's rule' implies a realm or sphere of existence where his authority is exer-
cised and recognized. Thus, Jesus speaks of 'entering into' the kingdom of God
(Lk. 16.16; 18.24; cf. Acts 14.22) and in terms that suggest that the Kingdom is
a realm (Lk. 7.28; 13.28).

[10] σωτήριον: Lk. 2.30; 3.6; σωτηρία: Lk. 1.69, 71, 77; 19.9; σῴζω: Lk. 6.9;
7.50; 8.12, 36, 48; 9.24; 13.23; 17.19; 18.26; 19.10; ἄφεσις: Lk. 1.77; 3.3; 4.18;
24.47.

of the realization that Jesus is the exalted Lord, not an abandonment of the kingdom as a present or future realm of blessing.[11] Certainly in Acts preaching the kingdom of God means to preach the gospel, the redemptive intervention of God in history in Jesus (Acts 8.12; 28.31). That the kingdom, as a realm of redemptive blessing, has a present dimension is indicated by the present experience of 'salvation' and 'forgiveness' for those who believe (Acts 2.47; 4.12; 11.14; 15.11; 16.31). In Acts, as in Luke's Gospel, 'salvation' (σωτήριον, σωτηρία, σώζω) and 'forgiveness' (ἄφεσις) are terms frequently used to describe redemptive blessings.[12] These terms are again associated with faith (πίστις).[13]

Thus, throughout Luke's two-volume work, the kingdom, as a realm of redemptive blessing, can be experienced in the present through faith in the proclamation of Jesus. Certainly a significant difference between Luke's Gospel and Acts is that in the former Jesus proclaims the message, whereas in the latter the disciples proclaim a message concerning Jesus. Yet this difference should not be overemphasized. In Acts, the mission that Jesus inaugurated and carried out in the power of the Spirit, is still the mission of Jesus (Acts 16.7), but it is now carried out by the church in the power of the Spirit. The preaching in Acts is still the preaching of the kingdom of the God (Acts 8.12; 14.22; 19.8; 20.25; 28.23, 31).[14] In both Luke and Acts entrance into the realm of God's redemptive blessings is contingent on a response of faith to Jesus. In the Gospel of Luke Jesus is present, calling for a response of faith. In Acts Jesus is still present, in the work of the Spirit through the disciples, calling for a similar response.

---

[11] Contra W.G. Kümmel and Otto Merk who maintain that the kingdom is not present during the church period (Kümmel, *Promise and Fulfillment*; O. Merk, 'Das Reich Gottes in den lukanischen Schriften' in Otto Merk, *et. al*, *Wissenschaftgeschichte und exegese: Gesammelte Aufsätze zum 65.Geburtstag* [*Beihefte zur Zeitschrift für die neutestamentliche*; Berlin: de Gruyter, 1998], pp. 272-91).

[12] σωτήριον: Acts 28.28; σωτηρία: Acts 4.12; 7.25; 13.26, 47; 16.17; 27.34; σώζω: Acts 2.21, 40, 47; 4.9, 12; 11.14; 14.9; 15.1, 11; 16.30, 31; 27.20, 31; ἄφεσις: Acts 2.38; 5.31; 10.43; 13.38; 26.18.

[13] Acts 10.43; 13.38-9; 14.9; 16.30, 31; 26.18.

[14] Youngmo Cho notes correctly that 'for Luke, to be a witness of Jesus means to bear witness to the kingdom of God' (Cho, *Spirit and Kingdom in the Writings of Luke and Paul: An Attempt to Reconcile these Concepts* [Paternoster Biblical Monographs: Milton Keynes: Paternoster, 2005)], p. 184).

In terms of the believers' experience of the kingdom, there is no difference between Luke and Acts. In both Luke's Gospel and the book of Acts entrance into this realm of God's rule constitutes salvation and is contingent on a response of faith to the proclamation of Jesus.

The Kingdom of God and the Content of Salvation

In Acts, as in the Synoptic gospels, the term, 'the kingdom of God' (ἡ βασιλεία τοῦ θεοῦ), can refer to a future eschatological realm of divine blessing (e.g. Acts 14.22). For Luke, this future realm is closely linked with the future resurrection (Lk. 14.14; 20.35). In Acts 4.2 Luke writes that the apostles 'were teaching the people and proclaiming in Jesus the resurrection of the dead' (ἐν τῷ Ἰησοῦ τὴν ἀνάστασιν τὴν ἐκ νεκρῶν). The force of the dative case ('in Jesus') is uncertain. It is possible to interpret ἐν τῷ Ἰησοῦ ('in Jesus') as a dative of reference, indicating that the content of the apostles' preaching included the resurrection of Jesus. The resurrection of Jesus was central to the preaching of the early church (Acts 2.32; 4: 9, 33; 26.23). However, it is also possible to interpret this phrase as an instrumental dative, with the apostles speaking of a future resurrection through faith in Jesus. This is most probable since the future hope of the early church clearly included the resurrection of the dead (Lk. 14.14, 20.35; Acts 24.15, 21). Luke 20.35 specifically connects the resurrection of the dead with the age to come. Acts 26.23 also indicates that the resurrection of Jesus is only the beginning, one that anticipates the resurrection of his followers as well. In light of these considerations it is evident that participation in the future resurrection of the righteous comprised part of the content of salvation, part of the future realm of divine blessings.

Although the actual resurrection of the body is a future event for Luke, entrance into the realm of divine blessing associated with this resurrection takes place in the present. This is vividly demonstrated by Luke's use of σῴζω ('to save') in the perfect and present tenses throughout Luke–Acts. In Lk. 7.50 Jesus declares to the sinful woman, 'Your faith has saved (σέσωκέν) you'. The perfect tense indicates that the woman experienced salvation at that point in time, although there were dimensions of her salvation that would be realized in the future. In Acts 2.47 Luke describes the growth of the early church in Jerusalem, 'The Lord added to their number daily those being saved (τοὺς σῳζομένους).' The present tense of σῴζω again indicates a present reception of salvation. For Luke, the present experience of salvation is preparatory for the future resurrection and the life of the age to come.

This is demonstrated further in the ethical content associated with entrance into the kingdom of God. Concern for the poor and the helpless will be rewarded at the resurrection of the righteous (Lk. 14.14). To be worthy of the kingdom involves making a radical, uncompromising decision to follow Jesus (Lk. 9.57-62; 14.26-35). In Acts, although the ethical implications of life in the kingdom are not a high priority, they are not altogether absent. In Acts 26.18 Luke records Paul's own account of his commissioning. He was commanded to go to the gentiles 'so that they might receive forgiveness of sins (ἄφεσιν ἁμαρτιῶν) and a place among those who are sanctified by faith in me.' Here, sanctification (i.e. the act of being set apart) is paralleled with forgiveness of sins and attributed to faith. Preparation for life in the age to come involves ethical transformation.

The present experience of salvation involves more than simply preparation for the future resurrection and life in the age to come. Through faith one actually enters into the realm of God's rule and blessings. For Luke, a result of faith in the message of Jesus is restored fellowship with God. Fellowship with God is an eschatological blessing associated with the future kingdom (Lk. 13.29; 14.16-24); yet, it is also a present experience for the disciples of Jesus (Lk. 22.27-30). The restoration of fellowship with God is the result of the divine ἄφεσις, a present experience (Lk. 7.48; Acts 10.43). In Acts 5.31 Luke records the testimony of Peter and the apostles concerning Jesus, 'God exalted him to his right hand as Prince (ἀρχηγὸν) and Savior (σωτῆρα) that he might give repentance and forgiveness of sins (ἄφεσιν ἁμαρτιῶν) to Israel.' The thought is this: Jesus is now in a position of authority, reigning at the right hand of God as Lord and Savior. By virtue of this authority Jesus is able to forgive sins. The preaching of the early church centered on the resurrection and exaltation of Jesus because this was so vitally linked to Jesus' present lordship and position of authority (Acts 2.33). This is why entrance into the future kingdom is contingent on a response of faith, for faith in the proclamation of Jesus involves the recognition of his present lordship by virtue of his resurrection and exaltation.

The Kingdom of God and Visible Signs

The salvation that is associated with the proclamation of the kingdom of God in Luke–Acts involves more than restored fellowship with God and ethical transformation. It is holistic in nature and impacts every aspect of our lives, both as individuals and as members of new 'kingdom' communities. Pedrito U. Maynard-Reid correctly notes, 'Luke shows that salvation is not limited to the personal, internal, spiritual realm … Healing, deliverance, and dramatic social change accompany' the proclamation of the kingdom throughout Luke–Acts.[15]

This was certainly the case in the ministry of Jesus. Jesus' healings and exorcisms, as well as transformed relationships, serve as dramatic evidence of God's decisive intervention and authority (e.g. Lk. 7.21-23; 19.7-9). They are signs that in Jesus God's rule is now being exercised. This is nowhere more clearly stated than in Lk. 11.20, where Jesus declares, 'But if I drive out demons by the finger of God, then the kingdom of God has come to you.'

It is important to note that Luke sees these visible and physical aspects of salvation also at work in the ministry of Jesus' disciples. First the Twelve and then the Seventy are commissioned to 'heal the sick' and proclaim that 'the kingdom of God is near' (Lk. 9.1-2; 10.9). This later commissioning of the Seventy echoes Moses' wish that 'all the Lord's people were prophets' (Num. 11.29) and thus points forward to Pentecost, when this wish begins to be fulfilled. It would appear that Luke sees the command to 'heal the sick' and 'proclaim the kingdom of God' as relevant for his church as well as the apostles. This conclusion is confirmed by the contours of Luke's narrative in Acts.

In order to assess the role of healing and visible signs in the narrative of Acts, we must begin with Peter's quotation of Joel's prophecy. Peter, quoting Joel 2.30-31, declares: 'I will show wonders in the heaven above, and signs on the earth below, blood and fire and billows of smoke. The sun will be turned to darkness and the moon to blood before the coming of the great and glorious

---

[15] Pedrito U. Maynard-Reid, *Complete Evangelism: The Luke–Acts Model* (Scottdale, PA: Herald Press, 1997), p. 106.

day of the Lord' (Acts 2.19-20). Joel's text only refers to 'wonders in the heavens and on the earth' (Joel 2.30). Yet Luke's skillful editorial work enables him to produce the collocation of 'signs and wonders' found in Acts 2.19. By simply adding a few words, Luke transforms Joel's text so that it reads: 'I will show wonders in the heaven *above*, and *signs* on the earth *below*' (Acts 2.19, added words in italics).

The significance of this editorial work becomes apparent when we read the verses that immediately follow the Joel quotation. Peter declares, 'Jesus ... was a man accredited by God to you by miracles, wonders and signs' (Acts 2.22). The significance of Luke's editorial work is magnified further when we remember that Luke also associates 'signs and wonders' with the ministry of the early church. In fact, nine of the 16 occurrences of the collocation of 'signs and wonders' (σημεῖα κὰι τέρατα) in the New Testament appear in the book of Acts.[16] Early in the narrative of Acts, the disciples ask the Lord to stretch out his 'hand to heal and perform miraculous signs and wonders' through the name of Jesus (Acts 4.31). This prayer is answered in dramatic fashion. A few verses later we read that, 'the apostles performed many miraculous signs and wonders among the people' (Acts 5.12). Similarly, Luke describes how Stephen, one outside the apostolic circle, 'did great wonders and miraculous signs among the people' (Acts 6.8). The Lord also enables Paul and Barnabas 'to do miraculous signs and wonders' (Acts 14.3; cf. 15.12).

All of this demonstrates that by skillfully reshaping Joel's prophecy, Luke links the miracles of Jesus and those of the early church together with the cosmic signs listed by Joel (Acts 2.19-20). Each of these miraculous events are 'signs and wonders' that mark these 'last days', that decisive period when God's rule begins to be realized on the earth. Luke, then, is not only conscious of the significant role that miracles played in the ministry of Jesus, he also anticipates that these 'signs and wonders' will continue to characterize the ministry of Jesus' followers, including those in his day.[17] According to Luke, healing and other visible manifestations of God's authority represent an integral and ongoing aspect of

---

[16] Acts 2.19, 22, 43; 4.30; 5.12; 6.8; 7.36; 14.3; 15.12.
[17] For a fuller discussion of 'signs and wonders', see Menzies, *Spirit and Power*, pp. 145-58.

the ministry of Jesus and his disciples. They are signs that the kingdom of God is invading this present age.

In short, Luke declares that the kingdom of God is inextricably linked to Jesus, who is Lord and Savior. The kingdom of God is none other than that realm of redemptive blessing where God's rule is exercised and acknowledged. As such, it represents salvation in all of its various aspects. This salvation has a future dimension, but it also can be experienced, in part, in the present through faith in the proclamation of Jesus. Jesus' proclamation of the kingdom included dramatic and visible signs of divine authority, such as healings, exorcisms, and radically altered relationships. Jesus commissioned his disciples to follow his example by healing the sick and proclaiming the kingdom of God as well. Jesus promised his disciples power to accomplish this task. The book of Acts narrates the fulfillment of this promise. Luke envisions that as his church proclaims the good news of the kingdom, which now centers on the death and resurrection of Jesus, visible manifestations of divine authority and liberation will also mark their ministry.

This brief survey of the kingdom concept in Luke–Acts raises significant questions concerning the attempt to translate ἐντὸς ἡμῶν with the phrase 'within you'. As we have noted, Luke nowhere describes the kingdom of God as something that is simply internal and spiritual. Quite the contrary, the kingdom of God is manifest in dramatic acts of healing and deliverance. It results in a radical reorienting of one's life that has visible and tangible results. Far from being an invisible and inner spiritual impulse, the kingdom of God is pictured as that realm where God's authority is exercised and acknowledged. I. Howard Marshall states the problem succinctly, 'Jesus speaks of men entering the kingdom, not of the kingdom entering men.'[18]

The evidence from the broader context of Luke–Acts (and, indeed, the entire synoptic tradition) suggests that the translation, 'within you', should be discarded. A better option is easily found. With a plural noun, as is the case in Luke 17.21, ἐντος can mean 'among' or 'in the midst of'.[19] Thus, the phrase in question would read, 'the kingdom of God is among you' or 'the kingdom of

---

[18] I. Howard Marshall, *The Gospel of Luke: A Commentary on the Greek Text* (NIGTC; Grand Rapids: Eerdmans, 1978), p. 655.

[19] See Marshall, *Luke*, p. 655 and the studies cited there.

God is in your midst' (Lk. 17.21).[20] This reading fits nicely into the teaching of Jesus as recorded in Luke–Acts. It is entirely compatible with Jesus' presentation of the kingdom of God as a realm in which God's rule is exercised, often in dramatic and visible fashion. As we have already noted above, a number of translations follow this line of interpretation.

However, the question must be asked, does this reading do justice to the immediate context of this saying in Luke's Gospel? To this question we now turn.

The Immediate Context: the Saying in Luke's Narrative

In Lk. 17.20-21 the Pharisees initiate the conversation by raising a question: when will the kingdom of God come? Jesus responds, 'The kingdom of God does not come with your careful observation, nor will people say, "Here it is", or "There it is", because the kingdom of God is among you.'[21] How are we to understand Jesus' response? At first glance it appears that Jesus is now denying what elsewhere is specifically affirmed in Luke–Acts: that the miracles of Jesus and the early church are signs of the presence of God's reign (Lk. 7.21-23; 11.20; Acts 2.19-22; cf. 2.43). However, in view of this larger context, we should probably understand Jesus' response in light of the prevailing messianic expectations current within Judaism. As Darrell Bock notes, although Judaism did not have a monolithic picture of the messiah's coming, 'in most conceptions it was a powerful and glorious arrival … the arrival of Messiah would be clear and obvious to all.'[22] By way of example, Bock cites Psalms of Solomon 17-18, where a powerful Messiah 'rules in Israel and rescues it from the nations'.[23] Clearly Jesus did not fulfill these expectations of a powerful, nationalistic leader who would bring political liberation to Israel. The recognition that Jesus does not fit conventional expectations is very likely reflected in Lk. 7.23, where Jesus responds to John the Baptist's question,

---

[20] In Chinese, *zhong jian* (中间). This reading is presented as a secondary option in the margin of the Chinese *Union Version*.

[21] I have altered the NIV by inserting 'among you' in the place of 'within you'. This reading is listed as a secondary option in the margin of the NIV.

[22] Darrell L. Bock, *Luke* (IVP NT Commentary Series; Downers Grove, InterVarsity Press, 1994), p. 286.

[23] Bock, *Luke*, p. 286.

'Are you the one who was to come?' After speaking of the blind receiving their sight, the lame walking, and lepers being healed, Jesus declares, 'Blessed is the man who does not fall away on account of me' (Lk. 7.23). There were indeed dramatic signs, but not the signs that many were seeking.

In Lk. 17.20-21 Jesus does not deny that visible signs accompany the coming of the kingdom; rather, he declares to the Pharisees that they are looking for the wrong signs. With his response, Jesus issues a warning: your attempts to calculate the correct time of the kingdom's arrival have failed, for the kingdom has already arrived – it is already in your midst and its source is standing before you – and yet you have failed to recognize it. Certainly here Jesus places the accent on the present-ness of the kingdom of God. The kingdom has already arrived in his person and thus it is now present in their midst.

This focus on the present-ness of the kingdom raises another crucial question: How then do we reconcile this saying with the future-oriented announcement that follows in Lk. 17.22-37? Surely the reference to the 'days of the Son of Man' (Lk. 17.22) refers to the consummation of the kingdom and the end of this present age. It would appear that Luke here has placed the twin emphases in Jesus' teaching on the kingdom of God, its surprising presence and its future fulfillment, in juxtaposition. Earle Ellis suggests that this alternating present/future perspective on the kingdom is characteristic of Luke and found repeatedly in his gospel.[24] In Luke's record of John the Baptist's prophecy the promise of a messiah who will baptize in the Holy Spirit finds a present fulfillment (Lk. 3.16), while the promise of fiery judgment refers to a still future event (Lk. 3.17). Jesus' warning of future rejection for those who are ashamed of him (Lk. 9.26) is followed by the promise that those standing before him will 'see the kingdom of God' (Lk. 9.27). Luke's version of the Lord's Prayer begins with the petition, 'your kingdom come' (Lk. 11.2), which is followed by the request for daily bread (Lk. 11.3; cf. 11.13, 20). In Lk. 12.37-46 references to future judgment are followed by sayings about immediate judgment. Finally, in Lk. 16.16 a saying concerning the

---

[24] E. Earle Ellis, *The Gospel of Luke* (revised ed, New Century Bible Commentary; Grand Rapids: Wm. B. Eerdmans, 1974), p. 210.

present proclamation of the kingdom is followed by a parable that speaks of future rewards and punishment (Lk. 16.19-31).

All of this indicates that we should not find it strange that Luke highlights the present-ness of the kingdom of God in a saying of Jesus that immediately precedes a prophetic oracle concerning the future coming of the Son of Man. This tension is common to Luke and appears to reflect his concern to provide an accurate and balanced perspective on Jesus' teaching concerning the coming of the kingdom of God. It is possible that Luke in this way seeks to encourage his readers, some of whom may have been discouraged by persecution. Luke reminds them that 'God's way of working in the world requires suffering from God's servants' and that those 'hopes which ignore this necessity are premature'.[25] An emphasis on the powerful presence of the kingdom of God coupled with a sober assessment of the challenges that will necessarily precede the consummation of God's redemptive plan would serve to encourage those in Luke's missionary communities as they seek to bear witness to Jesus in the face of opposition.

It is by now apparent that the translation 'among you' does justice to the immediate context of the saying as well as to the larger context of Luke–Acts. It also accords well with what we know about the actual historical setting of Jesus' ministry. This cannot be said for the alternative translation, 'within you'.

Conclusion

Although the NIV translates ἐντὸς ὑμῶν in Lk. 17.21 with the phrase 'within you' and the Chinese *Union Version* follows a similar approach, I have argued that this translation misses the mark. In Luke–Acts and the entire synoptic tradition Jesus never refers to the kingdom of God as an inner, invisible, and purely spiritual impulse. The notion that the kingdom of God is 'within you' runs counter to the way that the kingdom of God is presented throughout Luke's two-volume work. In Luke–Acts the kingdom of God is the dynamic realm of God's redemptive blessing where his rule is exercised and acknowledged. As such, the kingdom is

---

[25] Robert C. Tannehill, *The Narrative Unity of Luke–Acts: A Literary Interpretation, Volume 1: The Gospel According to Luke* (Philadelphia: Fortress Press, 1986), p. 257.

manifest in dramatic acts of healing and deliverance; and it results in a radical reorienting of one's life that has visible and tangible results. Jesus, as Lord and Savior, is the agent who brings the kingdom of God. Thus, the kingdom, as a realm of redemptive blessing, can be experienced in the present through faith in the proclamation of Jesus. 'Salvation' and 'forgiveness' are terms frequently used to describe these redemptive blessings. These blessings include restored fellowship with God and ethical transformation. However, the salvation that is associated with the proclamation of the kingdom of God in Luke–Acts involves more than this. It is holistic in nature and impacts every aspect of the disciple's life, both as an individual and as a member of a kingdom community. No wonder, then, that, 'Jesus speaks of men entering the kingdom, not of the kingdom entering men.'[26]

In the light of these considerations, I have suggested that we translate ἐντὸς ὑμῶν in Lk. 17.21 with the phrase, 'among you' or 'in your midst'. If we employ this translation, the text in question would read, 'the kingdom of God is among you' or 'the kingdom of God is in your midst' (Lk. 17.21).[27] This reading resonates nicely with the teaching of Jesus as recorded in Luke–Acts. It is entirely compatible with Jesus' presentation of the kingdom of God as a realm in which God's rule is exercised, often in dramatic and visible ways. Additionally, this reading fits well into the immediate context of Lk. 17.20-21. It serves to challenge the Pharisees' nationalistic and political understanding of the kingdom of God and it highlights the present-ness of the kingdom in a manner consistent with Luke's usage elsewhere.

It would appear that Pentecostals have read Lk. 17.20-21 rather well. Perhaps we should all follow their lead and joyfully celebrate God's awesome presence in our midst, his desire to heal, deliver, and transform lives. After all, the kingdom of God is in our midst.

---

[26] Marshall, *Luke*, p. 655.
[27] In Chinese, *zhong jian* (中间).

5

DID JESUS SEND SEVENTY OR SEVENTY-TWO?

While each of the synoptic gospels records a sending of the Twelve,[1] only Luke records a larger sending of disciples (Lk. 10.1-16). At this point in Luke's narrative (Lk. 10.1), every student of the New Testament is confronted with a perplexing question: How many disciples did Jesus send? The manuscript evidence is ambiguous: some manuscripts read 'seventy', while others list the number as 'seventy-two'. Since there is no consensus among scholars as to which reading should be considered authentic, translations vary. For example, the NIV states that 'the Lord appointed seventy-two' and sent them out (Lk. 10.1).[2] While other translations, such as the Chinese *Union Version*, list the number as seventy (*qi shi ge ren*).[3] In this chapter I would like to consider the question, how should we translate this text? As we consider this question, it will quickly become apparent that we are dealing with issues of far greater weight than a simple variation in digits. In fact, we shall discover that the numeric reference is full of symbolic meaning. It draws upon Old Testament imagery and in this way calls the reader to reflect upon dreams and promises from the ancient past. At the same time, this symbolic reference encourages the reader to anticipate the future fulfillment of these same dreams. All of this raises significant questions for the translator

---

[1] Mt. 10.1-16; Mk 6.6-13; Lk. 9.1-6.
[2] See also Lk. 10.17, where the number is listed again.
[3] 七十个人。

who wishes to convey these same nuances to contemporary readers.

The Lukan Context

Luke's account of the Sending of the Seventy (Lk. 10.1-16) is strategically located toward the beginning of Luke's travel narrative (Lk. 9.51–19.27). In this section of his gospel, Luke deviates from his tendency to follow Mark's chronology and appropriate Markan material. He now utilizes almost exclusively material drawn largely from Q or other sources unique to his gospel. The journey begins with Luke's declaration, 'Jesus resolutely set out for Jerusalem' (Lk. 9.51). In the ensuing verses references to the journey abound (Lk. 9.52, 57; 10.1, 38; 13.22; 14.25; 17.11). The portrait Luke generates is sharp and clear: Jesus, the eschatological prophet like Moses (Acts 3.22; 7.37; cf. Luke 4.18-19), embarks on a journey that will lead to Jerusalem and the inevitable fate of the prophet that awaits him there (cf. Lk. 11.47-51; 13.34; Acts 7.52). This journey 'on the way',[4] which has its counterpart in Acts with the movement of the disciples from Jerusalem to 'the ends of the earth' (Acts 1.8), takes on the character of a 'mission'.[5]

A number of elements in the journey foreshadow the church's mission to the Gentiles. Although Eduard Lohse perhaps overstates the matter when he maintains that Luke has crafted the narrative in order to give the impression that Jesus is traveling through Samaritan towns, he correctly notes several striking references to Samaritans along the way (Lk. 9.53; 10.33-37; 17.11, 16-19).[6] These references take on added significance if we see Luke deliberately omitting Q material reflected in Matthew 10.5-6, 'Do not go among the Gentiles or enter any town of the Samaritans. Go rather to the lost sheep of Israel.'[7] The Travel narrative is also filled with teaching material that reveals an inescapable truth: dis-

---

[4] For references to 'the way' (ὁδός) see Lk. 9.57; 10.4; 12.58; 18.35; Acts 9.2; 19.9, 23; 24.14, 22.
[5] Keith J. Hacking, *Signs and Wonders* (Nottingham: Apollos, 2006), p. 201.
[6] Eduard Lohse, 'Missionarisches Handeln Jesu nach dem Evangelium des Lukas', in *Die Einheit des Neuen Testaments* (Göttingen: Vandenhoeck & Ruprecht, 1973), pp. 178-92.
[7] Marshall, *The Gospel of Luke*, p. 413.

cipleship is inextricably related to mission (i.e. proclaiming the gospel to an, at times hostile, unbelieving world). Parables such as the Good Samaritan (Lk. 10.25-27), the Vineyard (Lk. 13.6-9), the Lamp (Lk. 11.33-36), the Watchful Servant (Lk. 12.35-48), the Great Banquet (Lk. 14.15-24), Tasteless Salt (Lk. 14.34-35), the Lost Sheep (Lk. 15.3-7), the Lost Son (Lk. 15.11-32), the Duty of a Servant (Lk. 17.7-10), and the Ten Minas (Lk. 19.11-27), all in various ways offer instruction that define discipleship in terms of mission. Other sayings, such as the cost of following Jesus (Lk. 9.57-62), the encouragement to pray for the Holy Spirit (Lk. 11.13; cf. Acts 1.8), the promise of the Holy Spirit's assistance when facing persecution (Lk. 12.11-12), and the promise of rewards for itinerant missionaries (Lk. 18.29-30), highlight related themes. The instructions that speak of one's use of possessions might also be placed in this category (Lk. 12.13-21, 22-34; 16.1-15, 19-31; 18.18-29; 19.1-9). It appears that Luke has selected and shaped the teaching material of the Travel Narrative so that it might encourage and guide the church as it engages in mission. It is reasonable to conclude, then, that in the Travel Narrative Luke presents Jesus as one who both models in his own life and offers instruction concerning the nature of the church's mission.

The Significance of the Seventy

With this context in mind, let us now turn to Luke's account of the Sending of the Seventy. As we have noted, all three synoptic gospels record Jesus' words of instruction to the Twelve as he sends them out on their mission. However, only Luke records a second, larger sending of disciples (Lk. 10.1-16). In Lk. 10.1 we read, 'After this the Lord appointed seventy-two [some mss. read, 'seventy'] others and sent them two by two ahead of him to every town and place where he was about to go.' A series of detailed instructions follow. The disciples are to pray for more workers, for 'the harvest is plentiful, but the workers are few' (10.2). Jesus warns the disciples that the journey will not be easy. They will face opposition, for he is sending them out 'like lambs among wolves' (10.3). The disciples are to travel lightly and with single-minded purpose. They are not to 'take a purse or bag or sandals', nor are they to 'greet anyone on the road' (10.4). When they enter a house, they are to utter a word of blessing, 'Peace to this house' (10.5). If they find a 'man of peace' there, one who is willing to show them hospitality, they are to stay there, eating and drinking whatever is offered (10.6-7). Similarly, if they are welcomed in a town, they are to eat what is offered (10.8). The group is then given this charge: 'Heal the sick who are there and tell them, "The Kingdom of God is near you"' (10.9). If the disciples are not welcomed, they are to issue warnings of impending judgment (10.11-15). Finally, Jesus reminds them of their authority, 'He who listens to you listens to me; he who rejects you rejects me; but he who rejects me rejects him who sent me' (10.16).

Our central question centers on the number of disciples that Jesus sent out and its significance. The manuscript evidence is, at this point, divided. Some manuscripts read 'seventy', while others list the number as 'seventy-two'. Bruce Metzger, in his article on this question, noted that the external manuscript evidence is evenly divided and internal considerations are also inconclusive. Metzger thus concluded that the number 'cannot be determined with confidence'.[8] More recent scholarship has largely agreed with Metzger, with a majority opting cautiously for the authenticity of 'seventy-two' as the more difficult reading.[9] Although we cannot determine the number with confidence, it will be important to keep the divided nature of the manuscript evidence in mind as we wrestle with the significance of this text.

Most scholars agree that the number (for convenience, we will call it 'seventy') has symbolic significance. A number of proposals

---

[8] Bruce Metzger, 'Seventy or Seventy-Two Disciples?', *New Testament Studies* 5 (1959), pp. 299-306 (quote, p. 306). See also the response of Sidney Jellicoe, 'St Luke and the 'Seventy (-Two)', *New Testament Studies* 6 (1960), pp. 319-21.

[9] All of the following scholars favor the 'seventy-two' reading as original: Darrell L. Bock, *Luke 9.51-24.53* (Baker Exegetical Commentary of the New Testament; Grand Rapids: Baker Academic, 1996), p. 994; Marshall, *Luke*, p. 415; Joel Green, *The Gospel of Luke* (NICNT; Grand Rapids: Eerdmans, 1997), p. 409; Robert C. Tannehill, *The Narrative Unity of Luke–Acts: A Literary Interpretation, Volume 1: The Gospel According to Luke* (Philadelphia: Fortress Press, 1986), p. 233; Craig Evans, *Luke* (New International Biblical Commentary; Peabody: Hendrickson, 1990), p. 172. One exception to this general rule is John Nolland, who favors the 'seventy' reading (Nolland, *Luke 9.21-18.34* [Word Biblical Commentary 35B; Dallas, TX: Word, 1993], p. 546.).

have been put forward,[10] but only two deserve serious considera-
tion. A majority of scholars find the background for the reference
to the 'seventy' in the list of nations in Genesis 10, which in the
Hebrew text numbers seventy and in the LXX, seventy-two.[11] The
number 'seventy' is then viewed as a symbolic anticipation of the
mission of the church beyond Israel to the Gentile nations. The
central reasons this position has been accepted by so many scholars are: (1) the theme of the Gentile mission is prominent in Acts
and there are specific parallels between the instructions given to
the seventy and the actual mission of the church as it is described
in Acts (e.g. the importance of table fellowship, traveling in
groups of two, and miracles of healing); and (2) the textual traditions for the table of nations (Hebrew: seventy; LXX: seventy-
two) account nicely for the divided manuscript evidence.

As compelling as these arguments appear at first sight, I would
suggest that the evidence points in another direction. The second
proposal, adopted by a minority of scholars,[12] maintains that the
background for the reference to the 'seventy' is to be found in
Num. 11.24-30. This passage describes how the Lord 'took of the
Spirit that was on [Moses] and put the Spirit on the seventy elders'
(Num. 11.25). This resulted in the seventy elders, who had gathered around the Tent, prophesying for a short duration. However,
two other elders, Eldad and Medad, did not go to the tent; rather,
they remained in the camp. But the Spirit also fell on them and
they too began to prophesy and continued to do so. Joshua, hear-
ing this news, rushed to Moses and urged him to stop them.
Moses replied, 'Are you jealous for my sake? I wish that all the
Lord's people were prophets and that the Lord would put his
Spirit on them!' (Num. 11.29). The significance of the symbolism

---

[10] For the various options see Metzger, 'Seventy or Seventy-Two Disciples',
pp. 303-304 and Bock, *Luke 9.51-24.53*, p. 1015.

[11] The following scholars favor this reading: Fred B. Craddock, *Luke* (Interpretation; Louisville: John Knox Press, 1990), pp. 144-45; R. Alan Culpepper,
The Gospel of Luke (The New Interpreter's Bible 9; Nashville: Abingdon Press,
1995), p. 219; Nolland, *Luke 9.21-18.34*, p. 558; Marshall, *Luke*, p. 415; Evans,
Luke, p. 169; Tannehill, *Luke*, p. 233; and Green, *Luke*, p. 412.

[12] Susan R. Garrett, *The Demise of the Devil: Magic and the Demonic in Luke's
Writings* (Minneapolis: Fortress Press, 1989), pp. 47-48, and Keith F. Nickle,
Preaching the Gospel of Luke: Proclaiming God's Royal Rule (Louisville: Westminster
John Knox Press, 2000), p. 114. Many scholars note this view as a possibility,
but cautiously opt for the table of nations (Genesis 10) explanation.

is thus found in the expansion of the number of disciples 'sent out' into mission from the Twelve to the Seventy. The reference to the Seventy evokes memories of Moses' wish that 'all the Lord's people were prophets', and, in this way, points ahead to Pentecost (Acts 2), where this wish is initially and dramatically fulfilled. This wish continues to be fulfilled throughout Acts as Luke describes the coming of the empowering Spirit of prophecy to other new centers of missionary activity, such as those gathered together in Samaria (Acts 8.14-17), Cornelius' house (Acts 10.44-48), and Ephesus (Acts 19.1-7). The reference to the Seventy, then, does not simply anticipate the mission of the church to the Gentiles; rather, it foreshadows the outpouring of the Spirit on all the servants of the Lord and their universal participation in the mission of God (Acts 2.17-18; cf. 4.31).[13] In Luke's view, each member of the church is called (Lk. 24.45-49; Acts 1.4-8/Isa. 49.6; cf. Lk. 11.13) and promised the requisite power (Acts 2.17-21; cf. 4.31) to engage in mission. Luke 10.1 anticipates the fulfillment of this reality.

The Numbers 11 proposal has a number of significant advantages over the Genesis 10 explanation. First, it should be noted that the Numbers 11 passage accounts for the two textual traditions underlying Lk. 10.1. While the number of the elders is listed in Num. 11.24-25 (cf. 11.16) as seventy, it is not entirely clear whether Eldad and Medad should be considered as part of the seventy or whether they are additions to the seventy. Thus, we can see why scribes would have been tempted to correct the 'seventy' to 'seventy-two', or vice versa. As we have noted, the Genesis 10 explanation also accounts for the two textual traditions. But neither the Hebrew nor the LXX text of Genesis 10 actually lists the number of nations as 'seventy' or 'seventy-two'. This number must be inferred from a calculation of the names included in the text. It is true that Jewish tradition lists the number of princes and languages in the world as seventy-two (3 Enoch 17.8; 18.2-3; 30.2), yet how clear this association would have been for Luke's audience is uncertain. In short, the Numbers 11 proposal, with its explicit reference to 'seventy' elders and a plausible explanation for scribal

---

[13] Nickle, *Luke*, p. 117: 'The "Seventy" is the church in its entirety, including Luke's own community, announcing the inbreaking of God's royal rule throughout the length and breadth of God's creation.'

discrepancies offers a clearer explanation of the textual tradition behind Lk. 10.1.

Secondly, the Numbers 11 proposal finds explicit fulfillment in the narrative of Acts, whereas the Genesis 10 explanation does not. The fulfillment of Moses' wish in Num. 11.29 is clearly described in Acts 2, particularly since the Pentecostal outpouring of the Spirit is specifically stated to be a fulfillment of Joel's prophesy (Acts 2.16-21). By way of contrast, Acts 'contains no hint that Luke thought of the Gentile nations as numbering seventy(-two).'[14] In fact, the list of nations that Luke actually gives (Acts 2.8-11) offers a far more restricted list of nations.

Thirdly, the verse that immediately follows the reference to the Seventy focuses on the great need for more missionaries: 'The harvest is plentiful but the workers are few. Ask the Lord of the harvest, therefore to send out workers into his harvest field' (Lk. 10.2). The call to pray specifically for more workers is particularly striking. This fits more closely with an emphasis on the universal nature of God's missionary call (all of God's people are called to engage in the mission) rather than an emphasis on a universal mission (to all people, including the Gentiles).

Fourthly, the Numbers 11 proposal ties into one of the great themes of Luke–Acts, the work of the Holy Spirit. Luke consistently presents the Spirit as the source of prophetic inspiration and, as such, as the driving force behind the mission of the church.[15] In Lk. 11.9-13, by modifying his Q material (cf. Mt. 7.7-11), Luke returns to this great theme and challenges his church to pray for the gift of the Spirit. The repetitive nature of the prayer envisioned and the fact that this call to prayer is addressed to disciples (and thus clearly anticipates the post-Pentecost location of Luke's church) reminds us that Luke has in mind here a prophetic anointing similar to that of Jesus described in Lk. 4.18-19 (cf. Lk. 3.21-22) and that of the early church described in Acts 2.17-21 (cf. Acts 2.1-4). This reference to the Holy Spirit in close proximity to the Sending of the Seventy passage further strengthens our argument. The significance of this connection is heightened further by

---

[14] Garrett, *Demise of the Devil*, p. 47.
[15] See Menzies, *The Development of Early Christian Pneumatology with special reference to Luke–Acts*, pp. 114-279.

the references to prayer that join the two passages together thematically (Lk. 10.3; 11.1-13).

Finally, a number of recent scholarly studies have noted that in his Travel Narrative, Luke 'presents Jesus as the prophet like Moses, on a journey to Jerusalem to effect a new Exodus for the people of God.'[16] The stage is set in the Transfiguration account (Lk. 9.28-36), where Moses, along with Elijah, appears in glorious splendor and speaks with Jesus (Lk. 10.30-31). They speak of Jesus' ἔξοδον ('departure'), 'which he was about to bring to fulfillment at Jerusalem' (Lk. 9.31). We can also hear an echo of Deuteronomy 18.15, 'The Lord your God will raise up for you a prophet like me from among your own brothers. You must listen to him [αὐτοῦ ἀκούσεσθε]', in the phrase, 'Listen to him [αὐτοῦ ἀκούετε]', found in Lk. 9.35. One need not accept in its entirety the theses of C.F. Evans or David Moessner, both of whom suggest that Luke structures his Travel Narrative largely on the basis of the book of Deuteronomy, to recognize that an interest in Moses typology has influenced Luke's literary program in a significant way.[17] Certainly we should not miss the fact that the words 'serpent' (ὄφις) and 'scorpion' (σκορπίος) which appear together in Lk. 10.19 are found together in the Old Testament (LXX) only in Deut. 8.15. And Luke's redacted version of the Q saying found in Lk. 11.20, 'But if I drive out demons by the finger of God [ἐν δακτύλῳ θεοῦ], then the kingdom of God has come to you', echoes Exod. 8.19 (8.15 LXX), 'The magicians said to Pharaoh, "This is the finger of God" [δάκτυλος θεοῦ].'[18] Luke's narrative also explicitly depicts Jesus as 'the prophet like Moses' (Acts 3.22; 7.37; cf. Deut. 8.15-19) who, like Moses before Pharaoh (Exod. 7.3), performs 'signs and wonders' (σημεῖα καὶ τέρατα; Acts 2.19).

---

[16] Greg W. Forbes, *The God of Old: the Role of the Lukan Parables in the Purpose of Luke's Gospel* (JSNTSup 198; Sheffield: Sheffield Academic Press, 2000), p. 329.

[17] So also Edward J. Woods, *The 'Finger of God' and Pneumatology in Luke–Acts* (JSNTSup 205; Sheffield: Sheffield Academic Press, 2001), pp. 47-48. Note also C.F. Evans, 'The Central Section of Luke's Gospel', in D.E. Nineham (ed.), *Studies in the Gospels* (Oxford: Blackwell, 1957), pp. 37-53 and David P. Moessner, *Lord of the Banquet: The Literary and Theological Significance of the Lukan Travel Narrative* (Minneapolis: Fortress Press, 1989).

[18] For arguments supporting the notion that Luke has altered the original Q reading, 'Spirit of God', reflected in Mt. 12.28, see Menzies, *Development*, pp. 185-89.

These allusions to Moses and his actions collectively add considerable support to our suggestion that the symbolism for Luke's reference to the Seventy should be found in Numbers 11 rather than Genesis 10.

Conclusion

The cumulative evidence is compelling and leads us to conclude that Luke has indeed crafted his account of the Sending of the Seventy with the seventy elders of Numbers 11 and particularly Moses' wish that 'all the Lord's people were prophets' (Num. 11.29) in mind. In this way, Luke anticipates Pentecost, when Moses' wish begins to be fulfilled. But Luke clearly looks beyond Pentecost to the needs of his own church (cf. Lk. 11.13). Just as Moses' wish continues to be fulfilled throughout the narrative of Acts as Luke describes the establishment of new centers of missionary activity in Samaria (Acts 8.14-17), Cornelius' house (Acts 10.44-48), and Ephesus (Acts 19.1-7), so also Luke anticipates that Moses' wish will be fulfilled in the lives of those in his church (cf. Acts 2.17-21). The Sending of the Seventy foreshadows the outpouring of the Spirit upon all the Lord's people and their universal participation in the mission of God. In Luke's view, every believer is called to take up Israel's prophetic vocation and be 'a light to the nations' by bearing bold witness for Jesus (Acts 1.4-8; cf. Isa. 49.6).

These conclusions have significant implications for the scholar wishing to accurately translate Lk. 10.1.[19] I believe that they help the translator move beyond the impasse created by uncertainty in the textual tradition. Indeed, if these conclusions are correct, then there are good reasons to take a pragmatic approach. Since the translator's aim is to enable contemporary readers to experience the text as much as possible like the original readers did, I would suggest that the number in Lk. 10.1 should be translated as 'seventy' rather than 'seventy-two'. For this number, specifically cited in Num. 11.24-25, most clearly draws the mind of the contemporary reader to consider the important events of the past (the experience of the elders in Numbers 11 and Moses' wish, which finds

---

[19] And, of course, Lk. 10.17, which refers to the same number.

initial fulfillment in Acts 2) and our future (will we witness for Jesus in the power of the Spirit?).

6

TONGUES OR LANGUAGES?

Numerous Protestant scholars have highlighted the unique nature of the Pentecostal outpouring of the Spirit recorded in Acts 2.[1] Pentecost, we are told, can never be repeated because it represents the birth of the church. The church has only one beginning, one birthday. Furthermore, this unrepeatable beginning takes place at a very special moment in salvation history. Never again will followers of Jesus pass through this unique period marked by Jesus' death, resurrection, and bestowal of the Spirit. At Pentecost, the disciples move into a new era.[2] The experience of successive generations of Christians, now shaped by our location in the age of the Spirit's availability, can never approximate that of the original 120. According to this perspective, then, the Pentecostal outpouring of the Spirit represents, to a large degree, that which is unrepeatable. We should not expect to see the various elements of the experience that are narrated in Acts 2 repeated in our day.

A recent example of this approach is found in Ben Witherington's commentary on Acts. Speaking of Pentecost, Witherington states that 'in crucial ways it is unique' and describes the event with non-inclusive pronouns: 'It is the empowering of *them* [the apostolic church] to do *their* job'.[3] For Witherington, then, the

---

[1] See for example Witherington, *Acts*, p. 132; J.R.W, Stott, *Baptism and Fullness: the Work of the Holy Spirit Today* (Downers Grove, IL: Inter-Varsity Press, 1975), p. 29; F.D. Bruner, *A Theology of the Holy Spirit: The Pentecostal Experience and the New Testament Witness* (Grand Rapids: Eerdmans, 1970), pp. 164, 169; James Dunn, 'Baptism in the Spirit: A Response to Pentecostal Scholarship', *Journal of Pentecostal Theology* 3 (1993), p. 2.

[2] James Dunn, 'Response', p. 2: Dunn insists that Luke intended 'to accord an unrepeatable eschatological significance to the events at Jordan and Pentecost'. According to Dunn, at Pentecost, the disciples enter into the new age.

[3] Witherington, *Acts*, p. 132.

Pentecost narrative and the experience it describes do not really serve as models for later Christians. They are unrepeatable. Generally, proponents of this reading of Acts insist that one of the unique and unrepeatable aspects of Pentecost is the miraculous gift of speaking in other tongues or languages (γλώσσαις, Acts 2.4).[4] Later descriptions of 'speaking in tongues' in Acts (λαλέω γλώσσαις, Acts 10.46, 19.6) highlight the significance and reality of a particular group's incorporation into the body of Christ. They, again, are distinct and unique events marking the historical expansion of the early church and, as such, should not be viewed as presenting a pattern that subsequent generations of Christians should seek to follow.[5]

Of course most Pentecostals, for reasons cited below, read the book of Acts differently. Yet, as Pentecostal scholar Jenny Everts points out, the Pentecostal position has, on occasion, been undermined by a misleading translation of Acts 2.4.[6] Everts notes that the phrase λαλεῖν ἑτέραις γλώσσαις in Acts 2.4 is translated as 'to speak in other tongues' in most English versions, including the NIV. However, the New Revised Standard Version (NRSV), translates λαλεῖν ἑτέραις γλώσσαις with the phrase, 'to speak in other languages'. According to Everts, this translation is misleading because 'the NRSV ... chooses to retain the translation "tongues" in the other two occasions γλώσσαις is used to refer to this phenomenon in Acts'.[7] This translation, then, inappropriately isolates the phenomenon of speaking in 'other languages' in Acts 2.4 from the phenomenon of speaking in 'tongues' which occurs later in Luke's narrative (Acts 10.46; 19.6). Luke's intent to link the 'tongues' of Pentecost together with the 'tongues' of Casearea (Acts 10.46) and Ephesus (Acts 19.6) through the use of similar language is obscured. Everts concludes, 'Contextual consistency in translation certainly ought to include

---

[4] See for example Bruner, *A Theology of the Holy Spirit: The Pentecostal Experience and the New Testament Witness*, pp. 164, 169.

[5] Stott, *Fullness*, pp. 32-34.

[6] Jenny Everts, 'Tongues or Languages? Contextual Consistency in the Translation of Acts 2', *Journal of Pentecostal Theology* 4 (1994), pp. 71-80. The basic idea for this chapter stems from her work and I wish to acknowledge my debt to her fine article.

[7] Everts, 'Tongues', p. 72.

consistency within the context of an entire book as well as individual passages'.[8]

For Chinese believers it is important to note that this same inconsistency in translation is found in the Chinese *Union Version*. In Acts 2.4 the *Union Version* translators render λαλεῖν ἑτέραις γλώσσαις as '*shuo qi bie quo de huà*',[9] which means 'to speak in the languages of other nations'. However, in Acts 10.46 and 19.6 they translate λαλέω γλώσσαις with a different phrase, *shuo fang yan*,[10] which means 'to speak in other tongues' (glossolalia) or 'to speak in a regional dialect'. This phrase, *shuo fang yan*, is the normal way that Chinese believers refer to speaking in tongues (that is, glossolalia). This term is also used to translate references to γλῶσσα or speaking in tongues in 1 Corinthians 12-14. So, both the NRSV and the Chinese *Union Version* translate the phrase, 'to speak in tongues' (λαλέω γλώσσαις), inconsistently. This is the case, even though as we have seen, this practice runs counter to the stated translation principles of the Chinese *Union Version*.[11]

Everts notes that the key theological concern involved in the translation of γλώσσαις in Acts 2.4 is 'not whether or not the disciples were speaking actual foreign languages'.[12] She acknowledges that most interpreters agree that the tongues of Pentecost involve the miraculous speaking of foreign languages that the disciples had not previously learned. According to Everts, the central question is this: How are the tongues of Pentecost related to the other occurrences of tongues in Acts? 'Are the tongues of Pentecost part of a unique historical event or are they part of an experience that is repeated in the lives of believers after Pentecost?'[13]

In the following essay I will argue that Everts has indeed raised a valid concern. Translations that obscure the connection between γλώσσαις in Acts 2.4 on the one hand and γλώσσαις in Acts 10.46 and 19.6 on the other, need to be reconsidered. More spe-

---

[8] Everts, 'Tongues', p. 73. Everts notes that a number of other English translations, including J.B. Phillips' paraphrase of the New Testament, Today's English Version, the Living Bible paraphrase, and the Jerusalem Bible, also render the λαλεῖν ἑτέραις γλώσσαις of Acts 2.4 as 'to speak in other languages'.

[9] 说起别国的话。

[10] 说方言。

[11] See our discussion of these principles in Chapter One.

[12] Everts, 'Tongues', p. 77.

[13] Everts, 'Tongues', p. 77.

cifically, I will argue that the common assumption that Pentecost represents a unique and unrepeatable event is, at best, misleading. On the contrary, Luke highlights the continuity between the experience of the disciples at Pentecost and that of Jesus that preceded it, as well as that of the various disciples that follow it. This conclusion suggests that translations that obscure these literary connections, misread Luke's theological intent. We shall develop our argument, first, by examining Luke's understanding of salvation history in relation to the working of miracles. A recent and significant study that supports the traditional interpretation of Pentecost as a unique and unrepeatable event, Keith Hacking's *Signs and Wonders, Then and Now*, will serve as our dialogue partner.[14] Secondly, we shall observe Luke's understanding of salvation history through the lens of his pneumatology. At this point we will interact with an older but important and representative work: W.B. Tatum's article, 'The Epoch of Israel: Luke I-II and the Theological Plan of Luke–Acts'.[15] Finally, we shall explore Luke's presentation of 'speaking in tongues' in an effort to determine whether he viewed this experience as a unique event or characteristic of the life of the post-Pentecostal church.

Salvation History and Miracles in Luke–Acts

In 1970 James Dunn published his widely influential critique of Pentecostal theology, *Baptism in the Holy Spirit*.[16] More recently, one of Dunn's PhD students, Keith Hacking, has attempted to provide something similar for the theology of 'signs and wonders' associated with the Third Wave movement. The term 'Third Wave' refers to a movement of the Spirit that began in the 1980s, subsequent to the earlier Pentecostal and Charismatic movements. This 'Third Wave' of the Spirit sparked a movement that was significantly impacted by John Wimber and which embraced many other conservative evangelicals who formerly had been dispensa-

---

[14] Keith Hacking, *Signs and Wonders, Then and Now: Miracle-working, Commissioning, and Discipleship* (Nottingham: Apollos/IVP, 2006).

[15] W.B. Tatum, 'The Epoch of Israel: Luke I-II and the Theological Plan of Luke–Acts', *New Testament Studies* 13 (1966-67), pp. 184-95.

[16] James D.G. Dunn, *Baptism in the Holy Spirit: A Re-examination of the New Testament Teaching on the Gift of the Spirit in Relation to Pentecostalism Today* (London: SCM Press, 1970).

tionalists and cessationists. According to Hacking, Third Wavers present the practice of healing and exorcism, what John Wimber calls 'doing the stuff', as ministries normative for the contemporary church. Central to Third Wave theology is not only the practice of Jesus himself, but also the mentoring and commissioning he gives to his disciples. Third Wavers emphasize that Jesus modeled and then commissioned his disciples to proclaim and demonstrate through signs and wonders the presentness of the Kingdom of God. Hacking seeks to examine the purported biblical basis for these Third Wave claims. He focuses particularly on the commissioning accounts and teaching on discipleship found in the synoptic gospels and Acts.

From the outset, Hacking's position is made clear. He chides Third Wavers for a simplistic, uncritical reading of the gospels. This 'uncritical' approach is marked by two major flaws, both of which flow from the Third Waves' relative lack of engagement with the fruit of modern biblical scholarship. First, Third Wavers tend to read the gospels as one, homogeneous whole and thus they fail to discern the distinctive theological perspective of each gospel writer. Additionally, Third Wavers fail to grasp, especially for Luke, the importance of the shift in the epochs of salvation-history, which diminishes their ability to understand the unique role of Jesus and the apostles and the miracles they wrought. In short, Hacking suggests that in the rush of their enthusiasm for things supernatural, Third Wavers have foisted their agenda upon the NT texts.

Hacking develops his critique by examining the commissioning accounts and teaching on discipleship found in Matthew, Mark, and then Luke–Acts. Matthew, we are told, presents Jesus as a Mosaic prophet who rightly interprets the law. Jesus passes on his 'authority to teach' to the disciples and this constitutes the 'heart of the Great Commission'.[17] Hacking grudgingly acknowledges that the 'authority' that Jesus confers on the disciples might also include authority over the demonic, but he insists that Matthew places far greater emphasis on authority to forgive sins, as well as to teach. Hacking concludes that Matthew's teaching on discipleship, which includes the important themes of suffering and perse-

---

[17] Hacking, *Signs and Wonders*, p. 100.

cution, the necessity of forgiveness, and the discipline of righteous living, indicates that the working of 'signs and wonders' was not a particularly important dimension of Christian discipleship for Matthew. One is only left to wonder, particularly in light of Matthew's clear association of 'authority' and charismatic ministry (e.g. Mt. 9.8, 10.1, 28.18), if Matthew and his community really felt that these obviously important themes and an emphasis on signs and wonders were mutually exclusive.

Mark too presents a rich picture of Christian discipleship, one that concentrates on much more than simply the ability to perform miracles. The weighty matters of discipleship are taken up by Mark in his central section. Here Mark teaches by describing the blunders of the disciples on the one hand, and the corrective teaching of Jesus on the other. Discipleship for Mark centers on 'utter commitment, a servant spirit, willingness to suffer and a focus … on doing the will of God'.[18] Additionally, Hacking suggests that the commissioning of the disciples to perform healings and exorcisms is not aimed at the entire Christian community, but rather applies only to Christians engaged in pioneer missionary activity.

This conclusion creates a tension with Hacking's earlier statement that 'Discipleship for Mark has mission as its purpose'.[19] This tension is never resolved, but intensified when we realize that the central section of Mark's gospel includes a story about the disciples' inability to exorcise a demon (Mk 9.14-29). After an implicit rebuke ('O unbelieving generation … how long shall I put up with you!'), Jesus exorcises the demon and then instructs the disciples concerning how these kinds of demons are to be cast out. Elsewhere in the central section this sort of misunderstanding and correction is cited by Hacking as Mark's method of instruction. On the basis of Hacking's earlier conclusions, one would envision that here Mark is instructing his church concerning the proper method of and approach to exorcism. Not so, declares Hacking. In an interesting bit of reverse logic, Hacking concludes that the story teaches 'that the earlier spectacular successes on the part of the disciples sent out by Jesus in mission should

---

[18] Hacking, *Signs and Wonders*, p. 152.
[19] Hacking, *Signs and Wonders*, p. 112.

not be regarded by Mark's readers as the everyday norm for the church'.[20] This puzzling hermeneutical shift continues with Hacking's analysis of Mk 9.38-41, which describes Jesus' correction of John, who is peeved that someone apart from the Twelve was casting out demons. Jesus declares,

> 'Do not stop him ... No one who does a miracle in my name can in the next moment say anything bad about me, for whoever is not against us is for us. I tell you the truth, anyone who gives you a cup of water in my name because you belong to Christ will certainly not lose his reward' (Mk 9.39-41).

It would appear that this story, which has impressive parallels to Num. 11.26-29, encourages the Twelve and, by extension, Mark's church, *not* to limit the casting out of demons to a select few. Yet Hacking gleans something rather different from this text. According to Hacking, the story teaches that 'exorcism in Jesus' name need not necessarily involve (true) discipleship and, as such, should be regarded by his readers as being of relatively minor importance'.[21]

Hacking's treatment of Luke–Acts, which is especially crucial for our purposes, follows a pattern that has now become rather predictable. First, he argues that Luke does not present Jesus' reception of the Spirit as a model for later disciples. This is the case in spite of overwhelming evidence to the contrary. Hacking ignores the fact that Luke has crafted his narrative in such a way as to stress the parallels between Jesus' reception of the Spirit at the Jordan and the disciples' reception of the Spirit at Pentecost: both receptions take place at the outset of their respective ministries; both experiences are accompanied by visible manifestations; both are interpreted as a fulfillment of OT prophecy in the context of a sermon that closely follows the event. Hacking's judgment at this point is impaired by his tendency to accept the notion that Luke has a rigid, fragmented view of salvation-history. Conzelmann's three-epoch view was discredited long ago, but Hacking still operates with a slightly modified version of Conzelmann's scheme. Martin Hengel gave voice to a virtual consensus in Lukan scholarship when he wrote some years ago that Conzelmann's

---

[20] Hacking, *Signs and Wonders*, p. 130.
[21] Hacking, *Signs and Wonders*, p. 133.

view 'that Luke divides history up into three periods … was nevertheless misleading … In reality, the whole double work covers the one history of Jesus Christ, which … includes the interval between resurrection and parousia as the time of his proclamation in the 'last days' (Acts 2.17)'.[22]

Unfortunately, this faulty presupposition also encourages Hacking to emphasize discontinuity between the charismatic ministry of Jesus and the apostles on the one hand, and ministry in Luke's church and ours on the other. Hacking frequently argues for the uniqueness of the miracles of Jesus and the apostles. He states that 'signs and wonders in Acts are to be understood as being instrumental in the formation of the infant church'.[23] Hacking builds on this by arguing that Luke restricts signs and wonders to a chosen few, a select group of designated individuals who are set apart and commissioned, initially by Jesus, but later by their local congregations. He concludes, 'Luke associated signs and wonders only with those who had a transparently authoritative role to play in the missiological progress of the church'.[24]

Yet these conclusions again run counter to the evidence from Luke–Acts. The sending of the 70 (Lk. 10.1-16) is a case in point. Hacking argues that the instructions given to the 70, which include 'heal the sick' (Lk. 10.9; cf. 10.17), were limited to the earthly ministry of Jesus and were 'not intended by Luke to provide an ongoing contemporary paradigm'.[25] However, as we have already noted, this text has important parallels to Num. 11.24-29 and should be read with Moses' declaration, 'I wish that all the Lord's people were prophets' (Num. 11.29), in mind. The manuscript evidence, divided as it is between a sending out of 70 or 72, attests to the fact that the early church understood the text in this way. The actual number of the elders who were anointed in Numbers 11 is somewhat ambiguous, depending on whether or not Eldad and Medad are included in the original 70. This accounts for later scribal discrepancies. This passage then, which expands the group of empowered disciples beyond the Twelve and echoes

---

[22] Martin Hengel, *Acts and the History of Earliest Christianity* (trans. J. Bowden; London: SCM Press, 1979), p. 59.
[23] Hacking, *Signs and Wonders*, p. 257.
[24] Hacking, *Signs and Wonders*, p. 257.
[25] Hacking, *Signs and Wonders*, p. 195.

Moses' wish for a prophethood of believers, finds its fulfillment in the Pentecostal outpouring of the Spirit.

Luke's concern to encourage his church to see the Pentecostal gift of the Spirit and the charismatic power that it provides as available to every believer is further emphasized in Lk. 11.9-13 (par. Mt. 7.7-11), where Luke alters the Q version of the saying to read 'Holy Spirit' rather than 'good gifts'. Luke's redacted version of this saying ('how much more will your Father in heaven give the Holy Spirit to those who ask him!') obviously anticipates the post-Easter experience of the church, since the gift of the Spirit was not bestowed until Pentecost. By contemporizing the text in this way, Luke stresses the relevance of the saying for the post-Pentecostal community to which he writes. He crafts his narrative so as to encourage his church – indeed, the entire church – to pray that they too might be empowered by the Pentecostal gift.

Finally, Luke could hardly have stated the matter more clearly than he does in Peter's sermon at Pentecost (see especially Acts 2.17-22). Peter declares to the amazed crowd that the events of Pentecost which they have just witnessed represent the fulfillment of Joel 2.28-32. The universality of the promise is highlighted in Acts 2.17-18 with the reference to 'all people' and the poetic couplets that follow (sons/daughters; young men/old men; men/women). The point is unequivocal: in the last days the Lord will pour out the Spirit on *all* of God's servants.

Equally important for this discussion is Luke's alteration of Joel's text in Acts 2.19. We have already noted that with the addition of a few words, Luke transforms Joel's text to read: 'I will show wonders in the heaven *above*, and *signs* on the earth *below*'. The significance of these insertions, which form a collocation of 'wonders' and 'signs', becomes apparent when we look at the larger context of Acts. The first verse that follows the Joel citation declares, 'Jesus ... was a man accredited by God to you by miracles, *wonders and signs*' (Acts 2.22). And throughout the book of Acts we read of the followers of Jesus working 'wonders and signs'. In this way, Luke links the miraculous events associated with Jesus (Acts 2.22) and his disciples (e.g. Acts 2.43) together with the cosmic portents listed by Joel (see Acts 2.19b-20) as 'signs and wonders' that mark the era of fulfillment, 'the last days'. For Luke, 'these last days' – that period inaugurated with Jesus' birth and leading up to the Day of the Lord – represents an epoch marked by 'signs and wonders'. This text indicates, then, that Luke is conscious of the significant role that miracles have played in the growth of the early church and anticipates that these 'signs and wonders' will continue to characterize the ministry of the church in these 'last days'.

This text also demonstrates that for Luke, the salvation history presented in his narrative cannot be rigidly segmented into discrete periods. The Kingdom of God (or the new age when God's covenant promises begin to find fulfillment) is inaugurated with the miraculous birth of Jesus (or, at the very latest, with Jesus' public ministry, which was marked by miracles) and continues to be progressively realized until his second coming and the consummation of God's redemptive plan. Acts 2.17-22 thus offers an important insight into Luke's view of salvation history. Pentecost is indeed a significant eschatological event, but it does not represent the disciples' entrance into the new age;[26] rather, Pentecost is the fulfillment of Moses' wish that 'all the Lord's people were prophets' (Num. 11.29; cf. Joel 2.28-29/Acts 2.17-18) and, as such, represents an equipping of the church for its divinely appointed mission. In short, in this crucial passage Luke stresses the continuity that unites the story of Jesus and the story of the early church. Luke's two-volume work represents the 'one history of Jesus Christ',[27] a fact that is implied by the opening words of Acts: 'In my former book, Theophilus, I wrote about all that Jesus began to do and to teach …' (Acts 1.1).[28]

One significant implication that flows from this insight is that the birthday of the church cannot be dated to Pentecost. Indeed, in his stimulating monograph, Graham Twelftree argues that, for Luke, the beginning of the church must be traced back to Jesus' selection of the Twelve. Twelftree declares, 'Luke would not call Pentecost the birth of the Church. For him the origins of the Church is in the call and community of followers of Jesus during

---

[26] Only by reading Luke–Acts through the lens of Pauline theology can Pentecost be construed as the moment when the disciples enter into the new age.

[27] Hengel, *Acts*, p. 59.

[28] Twelftree, *People of the Spirit*, p. 30.

his ministry'.[29] Furthermore, Twelftree asserts that 'the ministry of the Church is not seen as distinct from but continues the ministry of Jesus ....'[30] These conclusions, drawn largely from Luke's portrait of the apostles, are supported by Luke's citation of Joel's prophecy.

We have seen that numerous texts reflect Luke's view that 'signs and wonders' should and will characterize the ministry of the church throughout these 'last days'. Nevertheless, in the face of all this evidence, Hacking seeks to argue that Luke restricts the working of miracles to the apostles and a few heroes of the Spirit who received special commissions. Yet the very fact that Hacking has to expand the 'limited' group beyond the apostles to other heroes of the Spirit should give the reader pause. Other questions emerge as well: Are we really to understand the prayer of Acts 4.29-30 ('Enable your servants to speak your word with great boldness. Stretch out your hand to heal and perform miraculous signs and wonders ...') as limited to a select few? Philip was commissioned to help with the distribution of food, not pioneer churches, and yet miraculous signs accompany his proclamation in Samaria (Acts 8.6). How does this fit with Hacking's thesis? And, apart from the apostles and other heroes of the Spirit, what other characters could Luke use to make his point?

In short, Hacking raises interesting and important questions concerning the theology of 'signs and wonders'. His discussion of discipleship material in the synoptic gospels and Acts is often insightful and inspiring. Furthermore, he demonstrates that the gospel writers were not fixated on charismatic power, nor were they uncritical in their approach to the miraculous. But key aspects of his thesis – that the gospel writers were largely uninterested in 'signs and wonders' as a significant component of Christian discipleship, that the miracles of Jesus and the apostles were not intended to serve as models for the post-apostolic church, and that the commissioning accounts are relevant to only a select few who are specifically commissioned to engage in pioneer work – appear to be built on a selective reading of the text and faulty presupposi-

---

[29] Twelftree, *People of the Spirit*, p. 28.
[30] Twelftree, *People of the Spirit*, p. 28.

tions. Chief among the latter is the notion that Luke has a rigid, fragmented view of salvation-history.

Salvation History and the Spirit in Luke–Acts

Luke not only shows continuity throughout the era of fulfillment in his portrayal of miracles, he also highlights a similar continuity in his presentation of the Holy Spirit. A careful examination of Luke–Acts reveals that Luke consistently portrays the gift of the Spirit as a prophetic endowment that enables its recipient to fulfill a divinely ordained task.[31] From the very outset of his two-volume work, Luke emphasizes the prophetic dimension of the Spirit's activity. The profusion of Spirit-inspired pronouncements in the infancy narratives herald the arrival of the era of fulfillment (Lk. 1.41-45, 67-79; 2.25-32). This era is marked by the prophetic activity of John, the ministry of Jesus, and the mission of his church, all of which are carried out in the power of the Spirit. Filled with the Spirit from his mother's womb (Lk. 1.15, 17), John anticipates the inauguration of Jesus' ministry. By carefully crafting his narrative, Luke ties his account of Jesus' pneumatic anointing (Lk. 3.22) together with Jesus' dramatic announcement at Nazareth (Lk. 4.18-19), and thus indicates that the Spirit came upon Jesus at the Jordan in order to equip him for his task as messianic herald. Literary parallels between the description of Jesus' anointing at the Jordan and that of the disciples at Pentecost suggest that Luke interpreted the latter even in light of the former: the Spirit came upon the disciples at Pentecost to equip them for their prophetic vocation. This judgment is supported by the Baptist's prophecy concerning the coming baptism of the Spirit and fire (Lk. 3.16), for Luke interprets the sifting activity of the Spirit of which John prophesied as being accomplished in the Spirit-directed and Spirit-empowered mission of the church (Acts 1.5, 8). It is confirmed by Luke's narration of the Pentecost event (Acts 2.1-13), his interpretation of this event in light of his slightly modified version of Joel 2.28-32, and his subsequent description of the church as a prophetic community empowered by the Spirit. Whether it be John in

---

[31] See Robert Menzies, *Empowered for Witness: The Spirit in Luke–Acts* (JPTSup 6; Sheffield: Sheffield Academic Press, 1991), pp. 104-228.

his mother's womb, Jesus at the Jordan, or the disciples at Pentecost, the Spirit comes upon them all as the source of prophetic inspiration, granting special insight and inspiring speech.

This continuity in the work of the Spirit, outlined above, ties together Luke's two-volume work. It exposes the fallacy of attempts to separate in rigid fashion the events of Pentecost from the prior experience of Jesus at the Jordan or the latter experiences of the early church narrated in Acts. Additionally, 'there is no closing of one age (apostolic) and the initiating of another (post-apostolic) period'.[32] The mission of Jesus continues to be carried out by his Spirit-empowered disciples and Luke understands this mission to span 'the last days' (i.e. the era of fulfillment).

This presentation of Luke's pneumatology challenges the conclusions of a previous generation of scholars, particularly those influenced by Hans Conzelmann's rigid three-epoch scheme of salvation history.[33] One of the key weaknesses in Conzelmann's scheme is its inability to account for the material in Luke's infancy narratives.[34] This is particularly true of Luke's descriptions of the work of the Holy Spirit found there. Can the material from the infancy narratives be fitted into his scheme, or does it represent an insurmountable challenge to the validity of Conzelmann's approach? Twenty years ago, this was a pressing question.

Representatives of the former position included H.H. Oliver, who used the infancy material to support Conzelmann's conclusions with only minor modifications,[35] and W.B. Tatum, who arrived at similar conclusions by attempting to contrast the work of the Spirit in Luke 1-2 with the operation of the Holy Spirit elsewhere in Luke–Acts.[36] Tatum's article merits special attention since it centers on the work of the Spirit.

---

[32] Twelftree, *The People of the Spirit*, p. 29.

[33] Hans Conzelmann, *The Theology of St. Luke* (trans. G. Buswell; Philadelphia: Fortress Press, 1961).

[34] C.H. Talbert, 'Shifting Sands: The Recent Study of the Gospel of Luke', in J.L. Mays (ed.), *Interpreting the Gospels* (Philadelphia: Fortress Press, 1981), p. 202.

[35] H.H. Oliver, 'The Lucan Birth Stories and the Purpose of Luke–Acts', *New Testament Studies* 10 (1964), pp. 202-26.

[36] W.B. Tatum, 'The Epoch of Israel: Luke I-II and the Theological Plan of Luke–Acts', *New Testament Studies* 13 (1966-67), pp. 184-95.

According to Tatum, Luke 'uses the birth narratives to characterize that period in salvation history before the ministry of Jesus as the Epoch of Israel'.[37] In support of this claim Tatum attempts to distinguish between the work of the Spirit in the three epochs of salvation history: the epoch of Israel, the epoch of Jesus' ministry, and the epoch of the church. In spite of these divisions Tatum notes that the Spirit functions as the Spirit of prophecy in Luke 1-2 (epoch of Israel) *and* in Acts 2-28 (epoch of the church). The only distinction is that what was formerly limited to a few chosen individuals in the epoch of Israel is universally available in the epoch of the church.[38] This leads Tatum to conclude that 'the prophetic Spirit in the nativity stories recalls the role of the Spirit in the past history of Israel'.[39] Although this may be true, Tatum ignores the fact that the renewed activity of the prophetic Spirit, once prominent in the past history of Israel, is itself an indicator of the dawning of the messianic age.[40] Far from designating the events of Luke 1-2 as a 'period of preparation',[41] the activity of the prophetic Spirit marks the decisive transition in God's plan for the restoration of his people. Indeed, the profusion of prophetic activity inspired by the Spirit characterizes Luke 1-2 as a drama of fulfillment. The content of the prophets' proclamation reveals the true significance of the events related in the narrative. Thus, both the *form* and the *content* of prophecy herald the message: God is *now* fulfilling his promises of old. Only by ignoring the eschatological significance of the restoration of the gift of the Spirit and the prophecy which it produces can Tatum attempt to separate Luke 1-2 from the rest of Luke–Acts.

Tatum also argues that the Spirit motif in Luke 1-2 sets John apart from Jesus and places the former in the epoch of Israel.[42] Tatum's argument rests on his attempt to distinguish between the prophetic function of the Spirit in Luke 1-2 and the messianic function of the Spirit in the epoch of Jesus' ministry. This distinc-

---

[37] Tatum, 'The Epoch of Israel', p. 190.

[38] Tatum, 'The Epoch of Israel', p. 191.

[39] Tatum, 'The Epoch of Israel', p. 191.

[40] E. Ellis, *The Gospel of Luke* (NCB; London: Oliphants, Marshall, Morgan, & Scott, 1974), pp. 28-29.

[41] Ellis, *Luke*, p. 193.

[42] The fact that the births of both John and Jesus are announced as 'good news' (εὐαγγελίζομαι, Lk. 1.19; 2.10) should call for caution at this point.

tion is based on three observations: first, during his ministry Jesus is the sole bearer of the Spirit, this is in striking contrast to the profusion of the Spirit's activity elsewhere; secondly, while the passive forms of πληρόω (frequently used in Luke 1-2) suggest intermittent association, Jesus' relation to the Spirit (πλήρης, Lk. 4.1) intimates a more permanent connection; thirdly, following Schweizer, Tatum suggests that Jesus is no longer a Man of the Spirit, but is now Lord of the Spirit. It should be noted, however, that Tatum's initial point does not further his argument. The limitation of the Spirit to Jesus during his ministry does not indicate that the function of the Spirit has changed. Indeed, as we have noted above, the Spirit in relation to Jesus continues to function as the source of special revelation and inspired speech. Tatum's second point is mitigated by the fact that πλήρης πνεύματος ἁγίου is not applied exclusively to Jesus (Lk. 4.1), but is also a description used of various disciples in the epoch of the church (Acts 6.3, 5; 7.55; 11.24), an epoch in which by Tatum's own admission the Spirit functions as the Spirit of prophecy. The contrast Tatum attempts to draw between the intermittent or temporary character of the experiences of the Spirit recorded in Luke 1-2 and the permanent character of Jesus' experience of the Spirit breaks down when it is recognized that for John the gift of the Spirit of prophecy was permanent (Lk. 1.15, 76; 20.6) and, although the references to Jesus are less conclusive, in Acts the gift of the Spirit was clearly repetitive for the disciples (Acts 2.4; 4.8, 31).[43] Tatum's third point is also dubious. Luke 4.1, 14 will not support the claim that Jesus is 'no longer a Man of the Spirit, but is now Lord of the Spirit',[44] and, in any event, what is at issue here is not the function of the Spirit, but the status of Jesus and his relationship to the Spirit.

In short, Tatum does point to superficial differences in the activity of the Spirit in various stages of Luke's work: reference to the Spirit's activity is limited to Jesus during the period of his earthly ministry and the Spirit, as never before, is universally avail-

---

[43] R. Stronstad, *The Charismatic Theology of St. Luke* (Peabody, MA: Hendrickson, 1984), p. 4; Haya-Prats, *L'Esprit force de l'église. Sa nature et son activite d'après les Actes des Apôtres* (trans. J. Romero; LD, 81; Paris: Cerf, 1975), p. 198.

[44] Bovon, *Luc le théologien: Vingt-cinq ans de recherches (1950-1975)* (Paris: Delachaux & Niestlé, 1978), p. 226.

able in Acts. However, Tatum fails to demonstrate that these epochs mark a transformation in the *function* of the Spirit. In each
epoch the Spirit functions as the Spirit of prophecy. This fact and
the eschatological significance of the Spirit's return suggest that
Luke's pneumatology does not support a rigid three-epoch interpretation of Luke's scheme of salvation history; on the contrary,
Luke's pneumatology emphasizes the fundamental continuity that
unites his story of fulfillment.

This portrait of Luke's prophetic pneumatology, accenting as it
does the continuity that binds together the ministry of Jesus with
that of his disciples in Luke–Acts, has been largely accepted by
the current generation of scholars. Robert Banks acknowledges
this significant trend, 'In regard to Luke's general view of the
Spirit, there is a scholarly consensus that the Spirit is the primary
agent legitimating the mission, that in Acts it is largely the Spirit's
prophetic work, which involves an "empowering for witness", that
dominates, and that Luke shows little interest in the Spirit as the
source of spiritual, moral, or religious renewal in the individual as
such'.[45] This conclusion is not without significance for our inquiry
into the nature of speaking in tongues in Luke–Acts.

Salvation History and Glossolalia in Luke–Acts

If Luke views miracles and the prophetic enabling of the Spirit as
characteristic of the mission of Jesus, including that mission as it
is carried out through the lives of Jesus' disciples in the book of
Acts and beyond, how shall we view his references to speaking in
tongues? Does Luke present speaking in tongues as a unique and
unrepeatable historical phenomenon? Or is speaking in tongues
part of an experience that Luke anticipates will be repeated in the
lives of subsequent generations of Christians?

Tongues or Languages in Acts 2.4?

The phenomenon of speaking in tongues is described in numerous passages in the New Testament.[46] In 1 Corinthians 12-14 Paul

---

[45] Robert Banks, 'The Role of Charismatic and Noncharismatic Factors in
Determining Paul's Movements in Acts' in G. Stanton (ed.), *The Holy Spirit and
Christian Origins* (Grand Rapids: William B. Eerdmans, 2004), pp. 117-18.
[46] See 1 Corinthians 12-14; Acts 2.4, 10.46, 19.6; note also Mk 16.17 and
Rom. 8.26-27.

refers to the gift of tongues (γλώσσαις)⁴⁷ and uses the phrase λαλέω γλώσσαις to designate unintelligible utterances inspired by the Spirit.⁴⁸ The fact that this gift of tongues refers to unintelligible utterances (e.g. the glossolalia experienced in contemporary Pentecostal churches) rather than known human languages is confirmed by the fact that Paul explicitly states that these tongues must be interpreted if they are to be understood (1 Cor. 14.6-19, 28; cf. 12.10, 30).

In Acts 10.46 and 19.6 Luke also uses the phrase λαλέω γλώσσαις to designate utterances inspired by the Spirit. In Acts 10.46 Peter and his colleagues hear Cornelius and his household 'speaking in tongues and praising God'. Acts 19.6 states that the Ephesian disciples 'spoke in tongues and prophesied'. The literary parallels between the descriptions of speaking in tongues in these passages and 1 Corinthians 12-14 are impressive. All of these texts: (1) associate speaking in tongues with the inspiration of the Holy Spirit; (2) utilize similar vocabulary (λαλέω γλώσσαις); and (3) describe inspired speech associated with worship and prophetic pronouncements. Additionally, since 1 Corinthians 12-14 clearly speaks of unintelligible utterances and there is no indication in either of the Acts passages that known languages are being spoken, most English translations (including the NRSV) translate the occurrences of λαλέω γλώσσαις in these texts with reference to speaking in tongues. We noted that the Chinese *Union Version* translates in a similar fashion, using a phrase (*shuo fang yan*) that refers to regional dialects or, for contemporary Christians, glossolalia.

The references to γλώσσαις in Acts 2.1-13, however, raise interesting questions for those seeking to interpret and translate this passage. The first occurrence of γλώσσαις is found in Acts 2.3, where it refers to the visionary 'tongues of fire' that appear and then separate and rest on each of the disciples present. Then, in Acts 2.4 we read that those present were all filled with the Holy Spirit and began to 'speak in other tongues (λαλεῖν ἑτέραις γλώσσαις) as the Spirit enabled them'. This phenomenon creates confusion among the Jews of the crowd who, we are told, repre-

---

⁴⁷ 1 Corinthians 12.10; 12.28; 13.8; 14.22, 26.
⁴⁸ 1 Corinthians 12.30; 13.1; 14.2, 4, 6, 13, 18, 23, 27, 39.

sent 'every nation under heaven' (Acts 2.5). The crowd gathered in astonishment because 'each one heard them speaking in his own language' (διαλέκτῳ; Acts 2.6). These details are repeated as Luke narrates the response of the astonished group: 'Are not all these men who are speaking Galileans? Then how is it that each of us hears them in his own native language' (διαλέκτῳ; Acts 2.7-8)? After they list in amazement the various nations represented by the group, they declare, 'we hear them declaring the wonders of God in our own tongues' (γλώσσαις; Acts 2.11)!

Since Acts 2.11 clearly relates γλώσσαις to the various human languages of those present in the crowd, most scholars interpret the 'tongues' (γλώσσαις) of Acts 2.4 and 2.11 as referring to intelligible speech. The disciples are enabled by the Spirit to declare 'the wonders of God' in human languages that they had not previously learned. This reading of the text has encouraged the NRSV and the Chinese *Union Version* to translate γλώσσαις Acts 2.4 and 2.11 with the term 'language' and its Chinese equivalent.

However, it should be noted that this text has been interpreted differently. Some scholars, admittedly a minority, have argued that the 'tongues' (γλώσσαις) of Acts 2.4 refer to unintelligible utterances inspired by the Spirit.[49] According to this reading, the miracle that occurs at Pentecost is two-fold: first, the disciples are inspired by the Holy Spirit to declare the 'wonders of God' in a spiritual language that is unintelligible to human beings (i.e. glossolalia); secondly, the Jews in the crowd who represent a diverse group of countries are miraculously enabled to understand the glossolalia of the disciples so that it appears to them that the disciples are speaking in each of their own mother-tongues. Although this position may at first sight appear to be special pleading, as Everts points out, there are in fact a number of reasons to take it seriously.[50]

First, it should be noted that Luke uses two different terms, both of which can refer to language, in Acts 2.1-13: γλώσσαις (Acts 2.4, 11) and διάλεκτος (Acts 2.6, 8). The term διάλεκτος

---

[49] See Everts, 'Tongues', p. 74, n. 9 and the works she cites, the most recent being J.L. Sherrill, *They Speak with Other Tongues* (New York: McGraw-Hill, 1964), pp. 105-106.

[50] Everts, 'Tongues', pp. 74-75. I am largely dependent on Everts for the points that follow.

clearly refers to intelligible speech in Acts 2.6, 8 and it may well be that Luke is consciously contrasting this term with 'the more obscure expression of ἑτέραις γλώσσαις' in Acts 2.4.[51] Given the usage of the term, γλώσσαις, elsewhere in the New Testament, particularly when it is associated with the coming of the Holy Spirit, this suggestion is entirely plausible. Luke certainly had other options before him: he could have referred to languages in other ways, as the usage of διάλεκτος in Acts 2.6-8 indicates. However, in Acts 2.4 he chooses to use the term γλώσσαις, which reappears in similar contexts in Acts 10.46 and 19.6.

Second, it may well be that the phrase τῇ ἰδίᾳ διαλέκτῳ ('in his own language') modifies the verbs of hearing in Acts 2.6 and in Acts 2.8. This is certainly the case in Acts 2.8: 'How is it that each of us hears them in his own native language?' Everts notes that, if we read Acts 2.6 in a similar way, 'these two verses would imply that each individual heard the entire group of disciples speaking the individual's native language'.[52] All of this indicates that Luke may not be using γλώσσαις (Acts 2.4, 11) and διάλεκτος (Acts 2.6, 8) as synonyms.

Third, the major objection to this interpretation is the fact that in Acts 2.11 γλώσσαις is used as a synonym for διάλεκτος: 'we hear them declaring the wonders of God in our own tongues' (γλώσσαις). However, it should be noticed that in Acts 2.1-13 Luke may be intentionally playing on the multiple meanings of γλῶσσα (tongue). In Acts 2.3 the term refers to the shape of a tongue ('tongues of fire'). In Acts 2.11 it refers to a person's mother-tongue or native language. Given the term's usage elsewhere in the New Testament, is it not likely that Luke intended his readers to understand his use of the term in Acts 2.4 as a reference to unintelligible speech inspired by the Holy Spirit (glossolalia)?

Fourth, this reading of the text offers a coherent reason for the reaction of the bystanders who thought that the disciples were drunk. While it is hard to imagine the crowd reacting this way if the disciples are simply speaking in foreign languages; the crowd's

---

[51] Everts, 'Tongues', p. 75.
[52] Everts, 'Tongues', p. 75.

reaction is entirely understandable if the disciples are speaking in tongues (glossolalia).

In short, the evidence suggests that Luke's references to speaking in tongues (λαλέω γλώσσαις) in Acts 10.46, 19.6, and quite possibly (but less certain) 2.4, designate unintelligible utterances inspired by the Spirit rather than the speaking of human languages previously not learned. The crucial point to note here is that in Acts 2.4 γλώσσαις may mean something quite different from that which is suggested by the translation, 'languages'. The translation 'tongues' on the other hand, with its broader range of meaning, not only captures well the nuances of both possible interpretations noted above; it also retains the verbal connection Luke intended between Acts 2.4, Acts 10.46, and Acts 19.6. Everts' conclusion is thus compelling: 'There is really little question that in Acts 2.4 "to speak in other tongues" is a more responsible translation of λαλεῖν ἑτέραις γλώσσαις than 'to speak in other languages'".[53]

The logical corollary of this conclusion for Chinese Christians is that there is a better way to translate the λαλεῖν ἑτέραις γλώσσαις of Acts 2.4 into Chinese than the '*shuo qi bie quo de hua*'[54] offered by the Chinese *Union Version*. Probably the best approach would be to translate this key expression in Acts 2.4 with the phrase, *shuo qi bie zhong de fang yan*,[55] which can refer to speaking in different kinds of tongues (glossolalia), different regional dialects, or different languages. This would also preserve the connection with the *shuo fang yan* of Acts 10.46 and 19.6.

Another alternative is found in *The Today's Chinese Version* (*xian dai zhong wen yi ben*),[56] which translates the phrase in Acts 2.4 as '*shuo qi bie zhong yu yan*'.[57] Although this translation has a more narrow range of meaning and refers specifically 'to speaking in other languages', it does retain a verbal connection to Acts 10.46 and 19.6 by translating λαλέω γλώσσαις in these texts with the phrase, *ling yu* (spiritual language).[58] This translation is thus better

---

53 Everts, 'Tongues', p. 75.
54 说起别国的话。
55 说起别种的方言。
56 现代中文译本。
57 说起别种语言。
58 灵语。

than that found in the Chinese *Union Version*, but perhaps not as good as our suggested translation above.

Luke–Acts and the Role of Tongues in the Church

The importance of retaining the verbal connections between the γλώσσαις (tongues) of Acts 2.4, Acts 10.46, and Acts 19.6 should not be missed. This becomes apparent when we examine Luke's understanding of the role of tongues in the life of the church.

A close reading of Luke's narrative reveals that he views speaking in tongues as a special type of prophetic speech. Speaking in tongues is associated with prophecy in each of the three passages which describe this phenomenon in Acts. In Acts 2.17-18 (cf. Acts 2.4) speaking in tongues is specifically described as a fulfillment of Joel's prophecy that in the last days all of God's people will prophesy. The strange sounds of the disciples' tongues-speech, Peter declares, are in fact not the ramblings of drunkards; rather, they represent prophetic utterances issued by God's end-time messengers (Acts 2.13, 15-17). In Acts 19.6 the connection between prophesy and speaking in tongues is again explicitly stated. When Paul laid hands on the Ephesian disciples, the Holy Spirit 'came on them, and they spoke in tongues and prophesied'.

Finally, the association is made again in Acts 10.42-48. In the midst of Peter's sermon to Cornelius and his household, the Holy Spirit 'came on all those who heard the message' (Acts 10.44). Peter's colleagues 'were astonished that the gift of the Holy Spirit had been poured out even on the Gentiles, for they heard them speaking in tongues and praising God' (Acts 10.45-46). It is instructive to note that the Holy Spirit interrupts Peter just as he has declared, 'He [Jesus] commanded us to preach to the people and to testify that he is the one whom God appointed as judge of the living and the dead. *All the prophets testify about him* that everyone who believes in him receives forgiveness of sins through his name' (Acts 10.42-43).[59] In view of Luke's emphasis on prophetic inspiration throughout his two-volume work and, more specifically, his description of speaking in tongues as prophetic speech in Acts 2.17-18, it can hardly be coincidental that the Holy Spirit breaks in and inspires glossolalia precisely at this point in Peter's sermon. Indeed, as the context makes clear, Peter's colleagues are

---

[59] Italics mine.

astonished at what transpires because it testifies to the fact that God has accepted uncircumcised Gentiles. Again, the connection between speaking in tongues and prophecy is crucial for Luke's narrative. In Acts 2.17-18 we are informed that reception of the Spirit of prophecy (i.e. the Pentecostal gift) is the exclusive privilege of 'the servants' of God and that it typically results in miraculous and audible speech.[60] Speaking in tongues is presented as one manifestation of this miraculous, Spirit-inspired speech (Acts 2.4, 17-18). So, when Cornelius and his household burst forth in tongues, this act provides demonstrative proof that they are in fact part of the end-time prophetic band of which Joel prophesied. They too are connected to the prophets that 'testify' about Jesus (Acts 10.43). This astonishes Peter's colleagues, because they recognize the clear implications that flow from this dramatic event: since Cornelius and his household are prophets, they must also be 'servants' of the Lord (that is, members of the people of God). How, then, can Peter and the others withhold baptism from them? (Acts 10.47-48).

The importance of this connection in the narrative is highlighted further in Acts 11.15-18. Here, as Peter recounts the events associated with the conversion of Cornelius and his household, he emphasizes that 'the Holy Spirit came on them as he had come on us at the beginning' (Acts 11.15) and then declares, 'God gave them the same gift as he gave us ...' (Acts 11.17). The fact that Jewish disciples at Pentecost and Gentile believers at Caesarea all spoke in tongues is not incidental to Luke's purposes; rather, it represents a significant theme in his story of the movement of the gospel from Jews in Jerusalem to Gentiles in Rome and beyond.

Some might be tempted to suggest at this point that the special role that speaking in tongues plays as a sign in Acts 2 and Acts 10 indicates that, in Luke's view, this phenomenon was limited to these historically significant events in the early days of the founding of the church. This, however, would be to misread Luke's nar-

---

[60] Of the eight instances where Luke describes the initial reception of the Spirit by a person or group, five specifically allude to some form of inspired speech as an immediate result (Lk. 1.41; 1.67; Acts 2.4; 10.46; 19.6) and one implies the occurrence of such activity (Acts 8.15, 18). In the remaining two instances, although inspired speech is absent from Luke's account (Lk. 3.22; Acts 9.17), it is a prominent feature in the pericopes that follow (Lk. 4.14, 18-19; Acts 9.20).

rative. As a manifestation of prophecy, Luke suggests that tongues have an ongoing role to play in the life of the church. Remember, a characteristic of 'the last days' – that era of fulfillment that begins with the birth of Jesus and ends with his second coming – is that all of God's people will prophesy (Acts 2.17-18). The fact that Luke recounts various instances of the fulfillment of this prophecy that feature speaking in tongues encourages the reader to understand that, like 'signs and wonders' and bold, Spirit-inspired witness for Jesus, speaking in tongues will characterize the life of the church in these last days. To suggest otherwise runs counter to Luke's explicitly stated message, not to mention that of Paul (1 Cor. 14.39).

Luke not only views speaking in tongues as a special type of prophetic speech that has an ongoing role in the life of the church, there are also indications that he sees this form of exuberant, inspired speech modeled in the life of Jesus. Apart from the general parallels between Jesus and his disciples with reference to Spirit-inspired prophetic speech (e.g. Lk. 4.18-19; Acts 2.17-18), there is a more specific parallel found in Lk. 10.21: 'At that time Jesus, full of joy through the Holy Spirit, said, 'I praise you, Father, Lord of heaven and earth ….'

Luke provides an interesting context for this joyful outburst of thanksgiving. It occurs in response to the return of the Seventy from their mission. As we have already noted, the sending of the Seventy (Lk. 10.1, 17) echoes the prophetic anointing of the seventy elders in Numbers 11. Some scholars, such as Gordon Wenham, describe the prophesying narrated in Num. 11.24-30 as an instance of 'unintelligible ecstatic utterance, what the New Testament terms speaking in tongues'.[61]

On the heels of this passage, Luke describes Jesus' inspired exultation. Particularly important for our discussion is the manner in which Luke introduces Jesus' words of praise: 'he rejoiced in the Holy Spirit and said' (ἠαλλιάσατο ἐν τῷ πνεύματι τῷ ἁγίῳ κάι εἶπεν; Lk. 10.21).[62] The verb, ἀγαλλιάω (rejoice), employed

---

[61] Gordon Wenham, *Numbers* (Tyndale OT Commentary Series; Downers Grove, IL: Inter-Varsity Press, 1981), p. 109. I am indebted to my good friend, Grant Hochman, for pointing me to this reference.

[62] I am following the *American Standard Version* here for the English translation.

here by Luke is used frequently in the LXX. It is usually found in the Psalms and the poetic portions of the Prophets, and it denotes spiritual exultation that issues forth in praise to God for his mighty acts.[63] The subject of the verb is not simply ushered into a state of sacred rapture; he also 'declares the acts of God'.[64] In the New Testament the verb is used in a similar manner. The linkage between ἀγαλλιάω and the declaration of the mighty acts of God is particularly striking in Luke–Acts.[65] The verb describes the joyful praise of Mary (Lk. 1.47), Jesus (Lk. 10.21), and David (Acts 2.26) in response to God's salvific activity in Jesus. In Lk. 1.47 and 10.21 the verb is specifically linked to the inspiration of the Holy Spirit and in Acts 2.25-30 David is described as a prophet. This verb, then, was for Luke a particularly appropriate way of describing prophetic activity.

The reference in Acts 2.26 is especially interesting; for here, the verb ἀγαλλιάω is associated with the word γλῶσσα (tongue). In a quotation from Ps. 16.9 (Ps. 15.9, LXX), Peter cites David as saying, 'Therefore my heart is glad and my tongue rejoices (καὶ ἠγαλλιάσατο ἡ γλῶσσά μου) ….' This association of ἀγαλλιάω with γλῶσσα should not surprise us, for five of the eight references to γλῶσσα in Luke–Acts describe experiences of spiritual exultation that result in praise.[66] All of this indicates that, for Luke, ἀγαλλιάω and γλῶσσα, when associated with the inspiration of the Holy Spirit, are terms that describe special instances of prophetic inspiration, instances in which a person or group experiences spiritual exultation and, as a result, bursts forth in praise.

We conclude that Lk. 10.21 describes Jesus' prayer of thanksgiving in terms reminiscent of speaking in tongues: inspired by the Spirit, Jesus bursts forth in exuberant and joyful praise. Although it is unlikely that Luke's readers would have understood this outburst of inspired praise to include unintelligible utterances (i.e. glossolalia), the account does describe a relatively similar experience of spiritual rapture that produces joyful praise. What is

---

[63] R. Bultmann, 'ἀγαλλιάομαι', *TDNT*, I, p. 19; W.G. Morrice, *Joy in the New Testament* (Exeter: Paternoster Press, 1984), p. 20.

[64] R. Bultmann, , 'ἀγαλλιάομαι', p. 20.

[65] The linkage is made explicit in three out of four occurrences of the verb (Lk. 1.47; 10.21; Acts 2.26). The only exception is Acts 16.34.

[66] These five include: Luke 1.64, Acts 2.4, 2.26, 10.46, 19.6. The other three references to γλῶσσα are found in Lk. 16.24; Acts 2.3, 11.

abundantly clear is that Luke presents Jesus' Spirit-inspired prophetic ministry, including his bold proclamation and exultant praise, as a model for his readers,[67] living as they do, in these 'last days'.

Conclusion

We have argued that the common assumption that Pentecost represents a unique and unrepeatable event needs to be reconsidered. Luke's presentation of salvation history cannot be rigidly segmented into discrete periods. Through his programmatic quotation from Joel recorded in Acts 2.17-21, Luke declares that the era of fulfillment is inaugurated with the miraculous birth of Jesus (or, at the very latest, with Jesus' public ministry, which was marked by miracles) and continues to be progressively realized until his second coming and the consummation of God's redemptive plan. Pentecost is a significant eschatological event, but it does not represent the disciples' entrance into the new age nor is it the birth of the church; rather, Pentecost is the fulfillment of Moses' wish that 'all the Lord's people were prophets' (Num. 11.29; cf. Joel 2.28-29/Acts 2.17-18) and, as such, it represents an equipping of the church for its divinely appointed mission.

This conclusion is supported by Luke's narrative, which highlights the continuity that unites the story of Jesus and the story of the early church. Luke's two-volume work represents a unified history of Jesus Christ, a fact that is implied by the opening words of Acts: 'In my former book, Theophilus, I wrote about all that Jesus began to do and to teach ...' (Acts 1.1).

Luke shows continuity throughout the era of fulfillment in his portrayal of miracles, and he also highlights a similar continuity in his portrait of the Holy Spirit. A careful examination of Luke–Acts reveals that Luke consistently portrays the gift of the Spirit as a prophetic endowment that enables its recipient to fulfill a divinely ordained task. Whether it be John in his mother's womb, Jesus at the Jordan, or the disciples at Pentecost, the Spirit comes upon them all as the source of prophetic inspiration, granting

---

[67] Luke's emphasis on prayer, and particularly the prayers and prayer-life of Jesus, is widely recognized by contemporary scholars.

special insight and inspiring speech. This conclusion is not without significance for the contemporary church, for Luke views miracles and the prophetic enabling of the Spirit as characteristic of the mission of Jesus, including that mission as it is carried out through the lives of Jesus' disciples in the book of Acts and beyond.

This emphasis on continuity in Luke's presentation of salvation history also calls us to consider carefully the significance of the verbal connections between the γλώσσαις (tongues) of Acts 2.4, Acts 10.46, and Acts 19.6. Our analysis of the evidence suggests that Luke's references to speaking in tongues (λαλέω γλώσσαις) in Acts 10.46, 19.6, and quite possibly (but less certain) 2.4, designate unintelligible utterances inspired by the Spirit rather than the speaking of human languages previously not learned. This is important for it indicates that in Acts 2.4 γλώσσαις may mean something quite different from that which is suggested by the translation, 'languages'. The translation 'tongues' on the other hand, with its broader range of meaning, not only captures well the nuances of both possible interpretations (unintelligible utterances or human languages); it also retains the verbal connection Luke intended between Acts 2.4, Acts 10.46, and Acts 19.6. We have found Everts' conclusion to be compelling: 'There is really little question that in Acts 2.4 "to speak in other tongues" is a more responsible translation of λαλεῖν ἑτέραις γλώσσαις than "to speak in other languages"'.[68]

The logical corollary of this conclusion for Chinese Christians is that there is a better way to translate the λαλεῖν ἑτέραις γλώσσαις of Acts 2.4 into Chinese than the '*shuo qi bie quo de hua*'[69] offered by the Chinese *Union Version*. Probably the best approach would be to translate this key expression in Acts 2.4 with the phrase, *shuo qi bie zhong de fang yan*,[70] which can refer to speaking in different kinds of tongues (glossolalia), different regional dialects, or different languages. This would also preserve the connection with the *shuo fang yan* of Acts 10.46 and 19.6.

---

[68] Everts, 'Tongues', p. 75.
[69] 说起别国的话。
[70] 说起别种的方言。

Although Christians from various church families will continue to interpret the significance of the verbal connections between the γλώσσαις (tongues) of Acts 2.4, Acts 10.46, and Acts 19.6 differently, these connections in Luke's text should be retained in our translations. These verbal links are important, we have argued, because Luke views speaking in tongues as a special type of prophetic speech that has an ongoing role in the life of the church, and there are indications that he sees this form of exuberant, inspired speech modeled in the life of Jesus. Indeed, Luke presents Jesus' Spirit-inspired prophetic ministry, including his bold proclamation and exultant praise, as a model for his readers, living as they do, in these 'last days'.

CONCLUSION

Our study of various texts that deal with the work of the Holy Spirit or charismatic themes in the Chinese and English New Testaments has produced a number of significant conclusions. In Chapter One we examined the manner in which the translators of the Chinese *Union Version* translate the verb, 'to prophesy' (προφη-τεύω), in 1 Corinthians 12-14. Our analysis revealed that the translators of the Chinese *Union Version* deviated from their guiding principles when they translated this verb. They did not translate the verb consistently nor did they render literally this verb with obvious theological significance. Rather, they unconsciously foisted Calvin's view of prophecy as preaching onto the biblical text.

In Chapter Two we analyzed a number of passages where the *Union Version* translators have translated the term, πνεῦμα, as referring to the human spirit or related attitudes, when in fact the term should be understood as a reference to the Spirit of God. We established that the *Union Version* translators were uncomfortable with texts that refer to the Spirit of God speaking to, leading, or guiding followers of Jesus in very personal and subjective ways. This tendency is not unique to the Chinese *Union Version* and can also be found in some English translations.

In Chapter Three we dealt with the vexing question, how shall we translate the term, παράκλητος? I suggested that the numerous attempts to translate παράκλητος with vague, non-forensic titles such as 'comforter', 'exhorter', 'counselor', 'helper', and the Chinese *Union Version's* 'teacher' (*bao hui shi*), all miss the mark. The usage of the term in Greek literature, its location in the context of John's gospel, and John's pneumatological perspective all indicate that παράκλητος should be understood in a legal or forensic sense. Thus, the term 'advocate' represents a better translation.

In Chapter Four I examined Jesus' declaration, 'the kingdom of God is within you' (Lk. 17.21). Although the NIV translates ἐντὸς ὑμῶν in Lk. 17.21 with the phrase, 'within you', and the Chinese *Union Version* follows a similar approach, I argue that these translations need to be reconsidered. In Luke–Acts and the entire synoptic tradition Jesus never refers to the kingdom of God as an inner, invisible, and purely spiritual impulse. On the contrary, in Luke–Acts the kingdom of God is the dynamic realm of God's redemptive blessing where his rule is exercised and acknowledged. As such, the kingdom is manifest in dramatic acts of healing and deliverance; and it results in a radical reorienting of one's life that has visible and tangible results. With this in view, I have suggested that we translate ἐντὸς ὑμῶν in Lk. 17.21 with the phrase, 'among you' or 'in your midst'.

In Chapter Five we discussed an intractable textual question. In Lk. 10.1 the manuscript evidence is divided: How many disciples did Jesus send out, seventy or seventy-two? Which number should we use when we translate this passage? I argue that Luke has crafted his account of the Sending of the Seventy with the seventy elders of Numbers 11 and particularly Moses' wish that 'all the Lord's people were prophets' (Num. 11.29) in mind. In this way, Luke anticipates Pentecost, when Moses' wish begins to be fulfilled. He also looks beyond Pentecost to the needs of his own church (cf. Lk. 11.13). The Sending of the Seventy foreshadows the outpouring of the Spirit upon all the Lord's people and their universal participation in the mission of God. In Luke's view, every believer is called to take up Israel's prophetic vocation and be 'a light to the nations' by bearing bold witness for Jesus (Acts 1.4–8; cf. Isa. 49.6). All of this indicates that we should take a pragmatic approach and translate the number in Lk. 10.1 as 'seventy' rather than 'seventy-two.' For this number, specifically cited in Num. 11.24-25, most clearly draws the mind of the contemporary reader to consider the important events of Israel's past and our future in light of Pentecost.

Finally, in Chapter Six, I challenge the common assumption that Pentecost represents a unique and unrepeatable event. Luke's presentation of salvation history cannot be rigidly segmented into discrete periods. Through his programmatic quotation from Joel recorded in Acts 2.17-21, Luke declares that the era of fulfillment is inaugurated with the miraculous birth of Jesus and continues to be progressively realized until his second coming and the consummation of God's redemptive plan. Luke shows continuity throughout the era of fulfillment in his portrayal of miracles, and he also highlights a similar continuity in his portrait of the Holy Spirit. This emphasis on continuity in Luke's presentation of salvation history calls us to consider carefully the significance of the verbal connections between the γλώσσαις (tongues) of Acts 2.4, Acts 10.46, and Acts 19.6. The evidence suggests that Luke's references to speaking in tongues (λαλέω γλώσσαις) in Acts 10.46, 19.6, and quite possibly (but less certain) 2.4, designate unintelligible utterances inspired by the Spirit rather than the speaking of human languages previously not learned. This in turn indicates that in Acts 2.4 γλώσσαις may mean something quite different from that which is suggested by the translation, 'languages'. The translation 'tongues' on the other hand, with its broader range of meaning, not only captures well the nuances of both possible interpretations (unintelligible utterances or human languages); it also retains the verbal connection Luke intended between Acts 2.4, Acts 10.46, and Acts 19.6.

The corollary for Chinese Christians is that there is a better way to translate the λαλεῖν ἑτέραις γλώσσαις of Acts 2.4 into Chinese than the '*shuo qi bie quo de hua*'[1] offered by the Chinese *Union Version*. Probably the best approach is to translate this key expression in Acts 2.4 with the phrase, *shuo qi bie zhong de fang yan*,[2] which can refer to speaking in different kinds of tongues (glossolalia), different regional dialects, or different languages. This translation would also preserve the connection with the *shuo fang yan* (speaking in tongues) of Acts 10.46 and 19.6.

Our context does impact how we read a particular text. This is precisely why it is helpful to study and compare translations of the Bible produced in other cultural settings. This observation also explains why we benefit so greatly when we interact with and learn

---

[1] 说起别国的话。
[2] 说起别种的方言。

from Christians who live and serve in settings quite different from our own. In a striking essay penned some years ago, Ulrich Luz stated the matter clearly: 'It is important to protect Paul from the constraints of one's own church's tradition and thus discover him anew over against one's own established views.'[3] Luz concludes with this stirring challenge: 'Only when we discover what is new, strange, and other in the very familiar biblical text, and only when we allow ourselves to receive new insight from members of other confessions [and, I would add, Christians living in other contexts] ... will our reading of the Bible have a future.'[4] I trust that this book has encouraged the reader to take up this challenge.

---

[3] Ulrich Luz, 'Paul as Mystic' in Graham N. Stanton, Bruce W. Longenecker, and Stephen C. Barton, eds., *The Holy Spirit and Christian Origins: Essays in Honor of James D.G. Dunn* (Grand Rapids: William B. Eerdmans, 2004), p. 143.
[4] Luz, 'Paul as Mystic', p. 143.

BIBLIOGRAPHY

Banks, Robert, 'The Role of Charismatic and Noncharismatic Factors in Determining Paul's Movements in Acts' in Graham N. Stanton, Bruce W. Longenecker, and Stephen C. Barton (eds.), *The Holy Spirit and Christian Origins: Essays in Honor of James D.G. Dunn* (Grand Rapids: Eerdmans, 2004), pp. 117-30.

Barclay, William, *The Gospel of Luke* (The Daily Study Bible Series, revised ed.; Philadelphia, Westminster Press, 1975).

Beasley-Murray, G.R., *John* Vol. 1 (Word Biblical Commentary 36; Waco: Word, 1987).

Behm, J., 'παράκλητος', in *TDNT*, Vol. V, pp. 800-14.

Belleville, Linda, '"Born of Water and Spirit": John 3:5', *Trinity Journal* 1 (1980), pp. 125-41.

Billington, Anthony, 'The Paraclete and Mission in the Fourth Gospel', in *Mission and Meaning: Essays Presented to Peter Cotterell*, ed. A. Billington, T. Lane, and M. Turner (Carlisle: Paternoster Press, 1995), pp. 90-115.

Bock, Darrell L., *Luke* (IVP NT Commentary Series; Downers Grove, Inter-Varsity Press, 1994).

—*Luke 9.51-24.53* (Baker Exegetical Commentary of the New Testament; Grand Rapids: Baker Academic, 1996).

Bovon, F., *Luc le theologien: Vingt-cing ans de recherches (1950-1975)* (Paris: Delachaux & Niestle, 1978).

Broomhall, Marshall, *The Bible in China* (London: China Inland Mission and Religious Tract Society, 1934).

Brown, Raymond, *The Gospel According to John, 2 Vols.* (The Anchor Bible 29; Garden City, NY: Doubleday & Co, Inc., 1966).

Bruce, F.F., *Commentary on the Book of Acts* (NICNT; Grand Rapids: Eerdmans, 1984).

Bruner, F.D., *A Theology of the Holy Spirit: The Pentecostal Experience and the New Testament Witness* (Grand Rapids: Eerdmans, 1970).

Bultmann, R., 'ἀγαλλιάομαι', *TDNT*, I, pp. 19-21.

Burge, G., *The Anointed Community: The Holy Spirit in the Johannine Community* (Grand Rapids: Eerdmans, 1987).

Carson, D.A., *The Gospel According to John* (Leicester: Inter-Varsity Press, 1991).

Chiu, Wai-boon, 'Chinese Versions of the Bible', *China Graduate School of Theology Journal* 16 (January 1994), pp. 83-95.

Cho, Youngmo, *Spirit and Kingdom in the Writings of Luke and Paul: An Attempt to Reconcile these Concepts* (Paternoster Biblical Monographs; Milton Keynes: Paternoster, 2005).

Conzelmann, Hans, *The Theology of St. Luke* (trans. G. Buswell; Philadelphia: Fortress Press, 1961).

Craddock, Fred B., *Luke* (Interpretation; Louisville: John Knox Press, 1990).

Cullmann, O., *Christ and Time* (Philadelphia: Westminster, 1964).

Culpepper, R. Alan, *The Gospel of Luke* (The New Interpreter's Bible 9; Nashville: Abingdon Press, 1995).

Dunn, James D.G., *Jesus and the Spirit: A Study of the Religious and Charismatic Experience of Jesus and the First Christians as Reflected in the New Testament* (London: SCM Press, 1975).

—*Baptism in the Holy Spirit: A Re-examination of the New Testament Teaching on the Gift of the Spirit in Relation to Pentecostalism Today* (London: SCM Press, 1970).

—'Baptism in the Spirit: A Response to Pentecostal Scholarship', *Journal of Pentecostal Theology* 3 (1993), pp. 3-27.

Ellis, E. Earle, *The Gospel of Luke* (revised ed, New Century Bible Commentary; Grand Rapids: Wm. B. Eerdmans, 1974).

Ervin, Howard, *Spirit Baptism: A Biblical Investigation* (Peabody: MA: Hendrickson, 1987).

Evans, Craig, *Luke* (New International Biblical Commentary; Peabody, MA: Hendrickson, 1990).

Evans, C.F., 'The Central Section of Luke's Gospel', in D.E. Nineham (ed.), *Studies in the Gospels* (Oxford: Blackwell, 1957), pp. 37-53.

Everts, Jenny, 'Tongues or Languages? Contextual Consistency in the Translation of Acts 2', *Journal of Pentecostal Theology* 4 (1994), pp. 71-80.

Fee, Gordon D., *The First Epistle to the Corinthians* (NICNT; Grand Rapids: Wm. B. Eerdmans Publishing Company, 1987).

—'Translational Tendenz: English Versions and Πνεῦμα in Paul' in Graham N. Stanton, Bruce W. Longenecker, and Stephen C. Barton (eds.), *The Holy Spirit and Christian Origins: Essays in Honor of James D.G. Dunn* (Grand Rapids: Eerdmans, 2004), pp. 349-59.

Forbes, Greg W., *The God of Old: the Role of the Lukan Parables in the Purpose of Luke's Gospel* (JSNTSup 198; Sheffield: Sheffield Academic Press, 2000).

Garrett, Susan R., *The Demise of the Devil: Magic and the Demonic in Luke's Writings* (Minneapolis: Fortress Press, 1989).

Green, Joel, *The Gospel of Luke* (NICNT; Grand Rapids: Eerdmans, 1997).

Grudem, Wayne, *The Gift of Prophecy in 1 Corinthians* (Washington: UPA, 1982).

Gunkel, Hermann, *The Influence of the Holy Spirit: the Popular View of the Apostolic Age and the Teaching of the Apostle Paul* (trans. R.A. Harrisville and P.A. Quanbeck II; Philadelphia: Fortress Press, 1979; German Original, 1888).

Haacker, K., 'Einige Fälle von 'erlebter Rede' im Neuen Testament', *Novum Testamentum* 12 (1970), pp. 70-77.

Hacking, Keith J., *Signs and Wonders, Then and Now: Miracle-working, Commissioning and Discipleship* (Nottingham: Apollos/IVP, 2006).

Haya-Prats, Gonzalo, *L'Esprit force de l'église. Sa nature et son activité d'après les Actes des Apôtres* (trans. J. Romero; LD, 81; Paris, Cerf, 1975).

Hengel, Martin, *Acts and the History of Earliest Christianity* (trans. J. Bowden; London: SCM Press, 1979).

Jellicoe, Sidney, 'St Luke and the 'Seventy (-Two)', *New Testament Studies* 6 (1960), pp. 319-21.

Jenkins, Philip, *The Next Christendom: The Coming of Global Christianity* (Oxford: Oxford University Press, 2002).

Kärkkäinen, Veli-Matti, 'Theology of the Cross: A Stumbling Block to Pentecostal/Charismatic Spirituality?' in Wonsuk Ma and Robert Menzies (eds.), *The Spirit and Spirituality: Essays in Honour of Russell P. Spittler* (JPTSup 24; London: T&T Clark International, 2004), pp. 150-63.

Kümmel, W.G., *Promise and Fulfillment* (London: SCM Press, 1957).

Ladd, G., *A Theology of the New Testament* (edited by Donald A. Hagner; Grand Rapids: Eerdmans, 1993 revised edition).

—*The Presence of the Future* (Grand Rapids: Eerdmans, 1974).

—'The Kingdom of God – Reign or Realm?', *Journal of Biblical Literature* 81 (1962), pp. 230-38.

Lohse, Eduard, 'Missionarisches Handeln Jesu nach dem Evangelium des Lukas', in *Die Einheit des Neuen Testaments* (Göttingen: Vandenhoeck & Ruprecht, 1973).

Luz, Ulrich, 'Paul as Mystic' in Graham N. Stanton, Bruce W. Longenecker, and Stephen C. Barton (eds.), *The Holy Spirit and Christian Origins: Essays in Honor of James D.G. Dunn* (Grand Rapids: Eerdmans, 2004), pp. 131-43.

Marshall, I. Howard, *The Gospel of Luke: A Commentary on the Greek Text* (NIGTC; Grand Rapids: Eerdmans, 1978).

Maynard-Reid, Redrito U., *Complete Evangelism: The Luke-Acts Model* (Scottdale, PA: Herald Press, 1997).

Menzies, Robert, *The Development of Early Christian Pneumatology with special reference to Luke-Acts* (JSNTSup 54; Sheffield: Sheffield Academic Press, 1991).

—*Empowered for Witness: The Spirit in Luke-Acts* (JPTSup 6; Sheffield: Sheffield Academic Press, 1994).

Menzies, William, and Robert Menzies, *Spirit and Power: Foundations of Pentecostal Experience* (Grand Rapids: Zondervan, 2000).

Merk, Otto, 'Das Reich Gottes in den lukanischen Schriften' in Otto Merk, *et. al, Wissenschaftgeschichte und exegese: Gesammelte Aufsätze zum 65.Geburtstag* (Beihefte zur Zeitschrift für die neutestamentliche; Berlin: de Gruyter, 1998), pp. 272-91.

Metzger, Bruce, 'Seventy or Seventy-Two Disciples?', *New Testament Studies* 5 (1959), pp. 299-306.

Michaels, Ramsey J., *John* (NIBC 4; Peabody, MA: Hendrickson, 1989).

Milne, Bruce, *The Message of John* (BST; Leicester: Inter-Varsity Press, 1993).

Mittlestadt, Martin, *The Spirit and Suffering in Luke-Acts: Implications for a Pentecostal Pneumatology* (JPTSup 26; London: T&T Clark International, 2004).

Moessner, David P., *Lord of the Banquet: The Literary and Theological Significance of the Lukan Travel Narrative* (Minneapolis: Fortress Press, 1989).

Montague, George T., *The Holy Spirit: Growth of a Biblical Tradition* (New York: Paulist Press, 1976).

Morrice, W.G., *Joy in the New Testament* (Exeter: Paternoster Press, 1984).

Nickle, Keith F., *Preaching the Gospel of Luke: Proclaiming God's Royal Rule* (Louisville: Westminster John Knox Press, 2000).

Nolland, J., *Luke 9.21-18.34* (Word Biblical Commentary 35B; Dallas, TX: Word, 1993).

Oliver, H.H., 'The Lucan Birth Stories and the Purpose of Luke-Acts', *New Testament Studies* 10 (1964), pp. 202-26.

Osborne, Grant R., *Revelation* (ECNT; Grand Rapids: Baker Academic, 2002).

Packer, J.I., *Keep in Step with the Spirit* (Old Tappan, N.J.: Fleming H. Revell, 1984).

Rengstorf, K.H., 'μαθητής', *TDNT*, vol. 4, pp. 390-461.

Ridderbos, H.N., *The Coming of the Kingdom* (Philadelphia: Reformed and Presbyterian, 1962).

Robeck, C.M., 'Gift of Prophecy', *The New International Dictionary of Pentecostal Charismatic Movements*, Stanley M. Burgess and Eduard M van der Maas (eds.), (revised and expanded; Grand Rapids: Zondervan, 2002).

Schnackenburg, R., *God's Rule and Kingdom* (Montreal: Palm, 1963).

Schnelle, U., 'Paulus und Johannes', *Evangelische Theologie* 47 (1987), pp. 212-28.

Sherrill, J.L., *They Speak with Other Tongues* (New York: McGraw-Hill, 1964).

Smalley, Stephen S., *The Revelation to John: A Commentary on the Greek Text of the Apocalypse* (Downers Grove: InterVarsity Press, 2005).

Storms, Sam, *The Beginner's Guide to Spiritual Gifts* (Ann Arbor, MI: Servant Publications, 2002).

Stott, J.R.W., *Baptism and Fullness: the Work of the Holy Spirit Today* (Downers Grove, IL: Inter-Varsity Press, 1975).

Strandenaes, Thor, *Principles of Chinese Bible Translation As Expressed in Five Selected Versions of the New Testament and Exemplified by Matthew 5.1 and Colossians 1* (Coniectanea Biblica NTS 19; Stockhom: Almquist and Wiksell International, 1987).

Stronstad, R., *The Charismatic Theology of St. Luke* (Peabody, MA: Hendrickson, 1984).

Talbert, C.H., 'Shifting Sands: The Recent Study of the Gospel of Luke', in *Interpreting the Gospels* (ed. J.L. Mays; Philadelphia: Fortress Press, 1981), pp. 197-213.

Tannehill, Robert C., *The Narrative Unity of Luke-Acts: A Literary Interpretation, Volume 1: The Gospel According to Luke* (Philadelphia: Fortress Press, 1986).

Tatum, W.B., 'The Epoch of Israel: Luke I-II and the Theological Plan of Luke-Acts', *New Testament Studies* 13 (1966-67), pp. 184-95.

Turner, Max, *The Holy Spirit and Spiritual Gifts Then and Now* (Carlisle: Paternoster Press, 1996).

—*The Holy Spirit and Spiritual Gifts in the New Testament Church and Today* (Peabody, Mass: Hendrickson, 1998 revised edition).

Twelftree, Graham, *People of the Spirit: Exploring Luke's View of the Church* (Grand Rapids: Baker, 2009).

Wenham, Gordon, *Numbers* (Tyndale OT Commentary Series; Downers Grove, IL: Inter-Varsity Press, 1981).

Wesley, Luke, *The Church in China: Persecuted, Pentecostal, and Powerful* (AJPSSup 2; Baguio City, Philippines: AJPS Books, 2004).

Westcott, B.F., *The Gospel According to St. John* (Grand Rapids: Eerdmans, 1954).

Witherington III, Ben, *The Acts of the Apostles: A Socio–Rhetorical Commentary* (Grand Rapids: Eerdmans, 1998).

Wolter, M., 'Apollos und die ephesinischen Johannesjünger (Acts 18:24-19:7)', *Die Zeitschrift für die Neutestamentliche Wissenschaft* 78 (1987), pp. 49-73.

Woods, Edward J., *The 'Finger of God' and Pneumatology in Luke-Acts* (JSNTSup 205; Sheffield: Sheffield Academic Press, 2001).

Zetzsche, Jost, *The Bible in China: History of the Union Version or The Culmination of Protestant Missionary Bible Translation in China* (Monumenta Serica Monograph Series 45; Nettetal: Monumenta Serica. 1999).

INDEX OF BIBLICAL (AND OTHER ANCIENT) REFERENCES

Other Ancient References

INDEX OF NAMES

Other Books from CPT Press

R. Hollis Gause, *Living in the Spirit: The Way of Salvation* (2009). ISBN 9780981965109

Kenneth J. Archer, *A Pentecostal Hermeneutic: Spirit, Scripture and Community* (2009). ISBN 9780981965116

Larry McQueen, *Joel and the Spirit: The Cry of a Prophetic Hermeneutic* (2009). ISBN 9780981965123

Lee Roy Martin, *Introduction to Biblical Hebrew* (2009). ISBN 9780981965154

Lee Roy Martin, *Answer Key to Introduction to Biblical Hebrew* (2009). ISBN 9780981965161

Lee Roy Martin, *Workbook for Introduction to Biblical Hebrew* (2010). ISBN 9780981965185

Martin William Mittelstadt, *Reading Luke–Acts in the Pentecostal Tradition* (2010). ISBN 9780981965178

Roger Stronstad, *The Prophethood of All Believers* (2010). ISBN 9780981965130

Kristen Dayle Welch, *'Women with the Good News': The Rhetorical Heritage of Pentecostal Holiness Women Preachers* (2010). ISBN 9780981965192

Steven Jack Land, *Pentecostal Spirituality: A Passion for the Kingdom* (2010). ISBN 9780981965147

John Christopher Thomas, *Toward A Pentecostal Ecclesiology: The Church and the Fivefold Gospel* (2010). ISBN 9781935931003

Made in the USA
Charleston, SC
16 October 2010